AI PROMPT
ENGINEERING
POWER

Unlock AI Superpowers! Master Prompt Strategies **+** Free
Access to the Best Generative Tools.
Transform your creativity and productivity with cutting-edge AI.

Lucky N.

A Special Note for You

At the end of this book, you'll find a QR code that leads to a selection of top generative AI tools. A few of these will be referenced throughout the chapters, giving you the chance to explore them further and put into practice what you've learned.

I wish you an enjoyable and enriching read, and hope you make the most of these valuable resources!

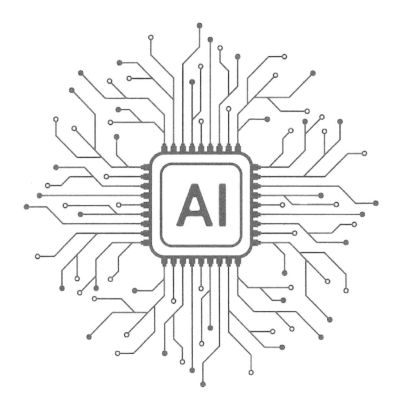

Luckyy.Nickyy@gmail.com

First Edition: January 2025

Table of Contents

The Need for Mastering Prompt Engineering in the AI Era

We are living in a time when artificial intelligence is no longer a distant concept but a transformative tool shaping industries, creativity, and daily life. Yet, the true power of AI lies in your ability to communicate with it effectively. Prompt engineering is the key to unlocking this potential—a skill that allows you to shape AI's responses, solve complex problems, and unleash innovation. Think of it as learning a new language, one that bridges human intent with machine precision. Mastering this craft means staying ahead in an era where AI proficiency defines success.

Real-Life Applications of Prompt Engineering

Prompt engineering isn't just a technical skill—it's a practical tool with tangible benefits. In content creation, it enables writers and marketers to produce tailored text quickly and efficiently. For customer support, AI chatbots can handle complex inquiries by responding accurately to well-crafted prompts, improving user experience. Developers use prompt engineering to generate code, automate debugging, and optimize performance. In healthcare, AI assists in data analysis and diagnostics, with precise prompts ensuring relevant and accurate results. From creative projects to business operations, mastering this skill allows you to harness AI's full potential, boosting productivity and driving innovation across various industries.

FOUNDATIONS OF AI AND PROMPT ENGINEERING

CHAPTER 1: WHAT IS PROMPT ENGINEERING?

In this chapter, we'll dive into the fundamental concept of prompt engineering, a key aspect of working with AI models. You'll learn what prompt engineering is, how it shapes the way AI models generate responses, and why the role of prompts is so crucial in extracting the most relevant and accurate outputs. Additionally, we'll explore real-life applications of prompt engineering, highlighting its significance across various industries. Whether you're just starting or refining your skills, understanding the basics of prompt engineering is essential for mastering the art of effective communication with AI.

DEFINITION AND KEY CONCEPTS

At its core, prompt engineering is the process of designing and refining input instructions—known as prompts—that you provide to an AI model to guide its behavior. Think of it as having a conversation with a highly intelligent system that can understand and generate language but needs you to set the context, tone, and direction. The clearer and more intentional your prompts are, the better the AI's response will align with your needs.

A prompt is not just a question or command; it's a carefully structured input that informs the AI what you expect. For example, asking, *"Summarize this article for a beginner in two sentences"* provides much more context and direction than simply saying, *"Summarize this."* This additional context helps the model focus its output, ensuring precision and relevance.

The key concept here is that AI models are not inherently "intelligent" in the human sense. They don't "think" or "understand" the way we do—they process inputs using probabilities based on patterns learned from vast amounts of data. Your role as a prompt engineer is to bridge this gap by providing instructions that the model can interpret effectively.

Another critical concept is **prompt specificity**. Vague prompts often lead to generic or incomplete responses, while detailed, well-defined prompts help the model deliver targeted results. For example, when creating content, specifying the tone, audience, and format can dramatically improve the outcome. Instead of saying, *"Write about climate change,"* you could say, *"Write a persuasive blog post about climate change, aimed at high school students, with a positive call to action."*

Equally important is the **iterative nature** of prompt engineering. Your first attempt at crafting a prompt might not yield the desired result, and that's okay. Learning to refine prompts based on the AI's output is a fundamental skill. By analyzing what works and what doesn't, you can gradually optimize your inputs to achieve better and more consistent results.

Finally, the concept of **contextual layering** is vital in more complex tasks. AI models work best when they are given the necessary background. For instance, before asking the model to write a detailed report, you might first supply it with relevant facts, data, or an overview to "prime" it for the task. This ensures that the AI operates with a foundation of knowledge tailored to your needs.

In essence, prompt engineering is a dynamic interplay between you and the AI. The better you understand its capabilities and limitations, the more effectively you can guide it to produce responses that align with your goals. It's both a science of precision and an art of creativity—a skill that evolves with practice and experience.

THE ROLE OF PROMPTS IN AI MODELS

Prompts are the bridge between human intention and machine response. They serve as the primary mechanism through which we communicate our needs to AI models, transforming abstract goals into actionable instructions the model can process. Without prompts, AI models would be aimless—capable of generating outputs but lacking the clarity to produce something meaningful or useful. Prompts, therefore, are not just tools; they are the foundation of how we unlock the potential of AI systems.

To understand their role, it's important to grasp how AI models, particularly large language models, work. These models are trained on immense datasets consisting of text from books, articles, websites, and more. They don't "understand" language in the way humans do, but they predict the most likely sequence of words based on the input they're given. A prompt acts as the starting point for this prediction process. It frames the model's task, setting boundaries and expectations for the output.

The effectiveness of a prompt lies in its ability to provide the model with context, intent, and structure. For instance, if you simply type, *"Explain gravity,"* the AI will attempt to generate a response, but the lack of specificity leaves much room for interpretation. Are you looking for a scientific explanation for adults? A simplified version for children? A technical paper for physicists? A prompt like, *"Explain the concept of gravity in simple terms, suitable for a 10-year-old,"* eliminates ambiguity, guiding the model to deliver a more precise and relevant response.

Prompts also play a critical role in defining the **scope and format** of an AI's output. When interacting with models, you're not just asking questions—you're setting the rules for engagement. For example, if you want the AI to write a marketing email, you can specify not just the content but also the tone (e.g., professional, friendly, humorous), length, and target audience. The more detail you include, the more the model can tailor its output to meet your expectations.

Another key aspect of prompts is their ability to **prime the model's knowledge**. AI models don't have memory in the human sense; they process each interaction as a standalone event unless you provide context within the prompt. For example, if you're working on a technical report and need the AI to analyze a dataset, you'll need to include that dataset or summarize its key points within the prompt. By doing so, you create a shared context that allows the AI to generate insights or conclusions relevant to your task.

Prompts also influence the **creativity and flexibility** of AI. A narrowly focused prompt can produce a highly specific result, while a more open-ended prompt can allow the model to explore creative possibilities. For example, asking the AI to *"Describe a futuristic city in detail"* might yield a rich and imaginative response, while adding constraints such as *"focused on sustainable architecture and energy systems"* narrows the output to a specific theme. The balance between creativity and control is determined entirely by how you craft your prompt.

Ultimately, prompts are the foundation of every interaction with an AI model. They define the relationship between user and machine, shaping how the AI interprets and responds to human intent. By understanding the pivotal role prompts play, you gain the ability to steer the AI effectively, ensuring it aligns with your goals and delivers meaningful results. As you refine your prompting skills, you'll discover just how transformative this process can be in leveraging the true power of AI.

REAL-LIFE APPLICATIONS OF PROMPT ENGINEERING

Prompt engineering is more than a theoretical concept; it is an actionable skill with tangible applications across industries and everyday scenarios. As AI continues to integrate into our lives, the ability to craft effective prompts is becoming indispensable, enabling you to harness the full potential of these systems. Let's explore how prompt engineering is being used in real-world contexts to drive efficiency, creativity, and innovation.

In **content creation**, prompt engineering has revolutionized how writers, marketers, and educators produce material. Imagine you're tasked with creating a blog post, social media captions, or even a detailed report. A well-designed prompt like *"Write a 500-word blog post explaining the benefits of renewable energy for beginners, in a conversational tone"* provides the AI with clear guidance, saving hours of effort while maintaining quality and relevance. For marketing professionals, prompts can help generate ad copy, product descriptions, or campaign slogans tailored to specific audiences, all while ensuring consistency in tone and messaging.

In **customer support**, AI-powered chatbots have become an essential tool for businesses, and prompt engineering is at the heart of their functionality. By designing prompts that anticipate user queries and guide the chatbot's responses, companies can create seamless and efficient customer experiences. For example, a prompt like *"If the customer mentions billing issues, ask for their account ID and summarize the issue before offering solutions"* ensures that the AI provides structured, helpful responses while reducing the workload on human agents.

The field of **software development** is another area where prompt engineering shines. Developers use AI tools to generate code snippets, debug errors, and even optimize algorithms. For instance, a prompt like *"Write a Python function to sort a list of dictionaries by a specific key"* allows developers to focus on higher-level problem-solving rather than repetitive coding tasks. This not only accelerates the development process but also improves productivity and innovation.

In **education and training**, AI can act as a personalized tutor or assistant, adapting to the unique needs of learners. Educators can design prompts such as *"Explain the Pythagorean theorem with a step-by-step example for a high school student"* or *"Create a 10-question quiz on World War II for middle school students"* to generate customized materials that enhance the learning experience. This adaptability allows for more engaging and effective education, whether in the classroom or online.

Even in **healthcare**, prompt engineering plays a critical role. Medical professionals can use AI to analyze patient data, draft reports, or assist in diagnosing conditions. For instance, a prompt like *"Summarize this patient's medical history and suggest potential risk factors for cardiovascular disease"* enables the AI to provide actionable insights that support decision-making, all while saving valuable time. While AI is no substitute for human expertise, well-crafted prompts ensure that the technology complements medical practices effectively.

In **creative fields**, such as art, storytelling, and game design, prompt engineering fuels innovation. Writers can use prompts to brainstorm story ideas, generate character descriptions, or outline plots, while game designers might leverage AI to create immersive dialogue or realistic world-building elements. For instance, asking, *"Describe a dystopian city where technology controls every aspect of life, focusing on visual details and atmosphere"* can produce imaginative and compelling results that spark creativity.

Even in **personal productivity**, prompt engineering proves its value. AI can assist with drafting emails, organizing schedules, or summarizing lengthy documents. A prompt like *"Summarize this 20-page report into a concise one-paragraph executive summary"* helps professionals save time and stay focused on strategic priorities. Similarly, AI can aid in brainstorming ideas or solving everyday problems, making it a versatile tool for personal and professional growth.

The common thread across all these applications is that the quality of the output directly depends on the quality of the prompt. Mastering prompt engineering enables you to tailor AI systems to your specific needs, whether you're automating routine tasks, enhancing creative processes, or driving innovation in your field. As AI continues to evolve, the demand for skilled prompt engineers will only grow, and those who master this skill will find themselves at the forefront of the AI revolution.

CHAPTER 2: UNDERSTANDING AI MODELS

In this chapter, we'll take a closer look at how AI models, particularly language models like GPT and other large language models (LLMs), work. You'll understand the key role that training data plays in shaping the behavior and output of these models. We'll also explore the evolution of AI, from early rule-based systems to the cutting-edge generative models we use today. By the end of this chapter, you'll have a clearer picture of how AI learns, processes information, and generates responses, laying a solid foundation for diving deeper into the intricacies of prompt engineering.

HOW LANGUAGE MODELS WORK (GPT, LLMS...)

Language models, particularly large language models (LLMs) like GPT, are at the forefront of AI advancements. These models are designed to process, generate, and understand human language in ways that mimic human-like conversation and problem-solving. To fully understand how they work, let's break down their inner mechanics, from the basic concepts to the cutting-edge technologies driving them.

At the core of every language model is a **neural network**—a mathematical structure inspired by the human brain's neurons and synapses. These networks consist of layers of interconnected nodes, each responsible for processing different aspects of the data. When we train an LLM, we feed it a massive amount of text data, teaching it to recognize patterns and relationships between words, phrases, and even entire sentences.

The **training process** involves exposing the model to billions of words and sentences across diverse contexts—books, websites, articles, conversations, and more. The goal is for the model to learn the statistical relationships between words and understand how they fit into different structures of meaning. Essentially, it learns by predicting the next word in a sentence, refining its predictions over time as it analyzes vast amounts of data.

One crucial component in language models like GPT (Generative Pre-trained Transformer) is the **transformer architecture**, which fundamentally changed the way AI handles language. The transformer model uses a mechanism called **attention** to focus on the most relevant parts of the input when generating output. This means the model doesn't treat all words or phrases equally but dynamically shifts its focus to the most important words in the given context. For example, if you're asking about the capital of France, the model knows to give extra attention to "capital" and "France" rather than wasting attention on less relevant words.

This attention mechanism is what allows these models to handle long-range dependencies in text, making them particularly effective at understanding complex sentences or multi-step tasks. Without attention, the model might struggle to grasp connections between words that are far apart, leading to disjointed or irrelevant responses.

Once trained, the model's ability to generate coherent, context-aware text stems from **predictive algorithms**. Given a prompt, the model generates a series of probabilities for the next word or phrase, then selects the most likely outcome. The model doesn't "understand" the meaning of words like a human does, but it generates the next word based on patterns and probabilities learned from the training data. For instance, if asked to continue the sentence, *"The sun sets in the..."*, the model might predict "west" based on the context of the sentence and prior knowledge from training.

A key advantage of these models is their **pre-training** phase. During pre-training, the model is exposed to general language data without a specific goal. This phase allows it to learn basic language rules, grammar, and structure. After this, the model goes through a process called **fine-tuning**, where it is further trained on more specialized data to improve its performance in specific tasks, like writing articles or answering technical questions. Fine-tuning helps refine the model's ability to generate more accurate, context-appropriate responses for particular applications.

LLMs like GPT can also be **scalable**, meaning they become more powerful as they're exposed to more data and increase in size. The larger the model, the more parameters it has—essentially the more "knowledge" it can store. This allows for greater flexibility and accuracy in the model's output. For instance, a smaller model might be limited in its ability to provide detailed answers, while a large-scale model like GPT-4 has a much broader understanding of various topics, from science to history to everyday conversation.

Beyond just GPT, there are many other language models that offer unique features and capabilities. Some models, like **BERT (Bidirectional Encoder Representations from Transformers)**, are optimized for understanding the context in both directions—

reading not just from left to right but also right to left, improving its comprehension of meaning. Others, such as **T5 (Text-to-Text Transfer Transformer)**, are designed to treat all tasks as text-to-text transformations, which means they can be used for everything from translation to summarization to question answering.

One of the most exciting aspects of these models is their **ability to generalize**. Unlike traditional algorithms that need specific rules or pre-programmed instructions, LLMs can take a prompt (a sentence or series of sentences) and generate output that fits the given context. This generalization ability is what allows them to excel across a wide range of tasks without needing explicit programming for each new situation.

For example, if you ask a GPT model to write a poem, it doesn't need to follow a rigid set of pre-defined poetic rules. Instead, based on its training, it can generate a creative, contextually appropriate response that resembles a human-written poem. Similarly, if you ask it for a technical explanation of a scientific concept, it will draw upon its knowledge of that subject, structuring the response in a way that makes sense for the task at hand.

However, despite their power, LLMs are not without limitations. While they excel at predicting the next word or generating coherent text, they lack true **understanding**. They don't "know" the meaning of the words they generate, nor do they have a genuine grasp of the world. They can provide plausible-sounding responses, but these responses are based on patterns rather than factual knowledge. This is why, when using LLMs, the quality of the input prompt is crucial. A poorly constructed prompt can lead to irrelevant or inaccurate results, while a well-crafted one can guide the model to generate insightful, high-quality text.

In conclusion, language models like GPT and other LLMs have transformed the landscape of AI by enabling machines to interact with human language in sophisticated ways. Their ability to process large amounts of text, predict patterns, and generate coherent responses is a result of complex architectures, massive training datasets, and cutting-edge algorithms. As these models continue to evolve, their potential to revolutionize industries—from content creation to healthcare to customer service—becomes increasingly apparent. Understanding how these models work is essential to leveraging their full capabilities and effectively utilizing prompt engineering to generate meaningful, accurate output.

TRAINING DATA AND ITS IMPORTANCE

Training data is the lifeblood of any AI model, shaping its capabilities, limitations, and overall behavior. Without a carefully curated dataset, even the most advanced language model cannot function effectively. But why is training data so critical, and how does it influence the performance of models like GPT?

At its core, training data serves as the foundation upon which an AI learns to understand and generate language. Think of it as the model's "education." By exposing the system to massive volumes of text—ranging from books and scientific papers to blogs and social media posts—the model learns patterns, relationships, and structures inherent in human communication. These patterns allow it to predict the next word in a sequence, craft coherent paragraphs, and even generate creative responses to abstract queries.

The diversity and quality of the training data are key. A model trained on narrow, biased, or outdated datasets will produce outputs that reflect those limitations. For example, if a dataset over-represents formal language but lacks conversational tones, the model may struggle to generate casual, natural dialogue. Similarly, if the training data excludes certain perspectives or cultures, the outputs may unintentionally perpetuate biases. This is why the selection and preparation of training data require meticulous attention.

Equally important is the **scale of the data**. Large language models are trained on billions of tokens to ensure they encounter a broad spectrum of language usage. This scale enables them to generalize effectively, understanding everything from colloquial slang to technical jargon. However, bigger isn't always better. Training on excessively large datasets can introduce noise or irrelevant information, reducing the model's accuracy and focus. Balancing breadth and relevance is essential.

Training data also affects the model's **contextual understanding**. By exposing the system to diverse scenarios, it learns to grasp nuances like humor, sarcasm, and ambiguity. For instance, a sentence like "That's just great" can be interpreted as genuine praise or sarcasm depending on context. Without sufficient examples of both usages, the model might misinterpret such subtleties.

Preprocessing is another critical step in handling training data. Raw text from the internet or other sources often contains inconsistencies, errors, and unnecessary information. Cleaning and structuring the data—removing duplicates, filtering low-quality text, and standardizing formats—ensures that the model trains on accurate and meaningful content. This preprocessing phase minimizes the risk of the model generating irrelevant or incoherent outputs later on.

The importance of training data extends beyond the model's initial capabilities. It also impacts **fine-tuning**, where the base model is further trained on domain-specific datasets to enhance its performance for particular applications. For example, a general-purpose language model can be fine-tuned with medical literature to assist healthcare professionals or with legal texts to support lawyers. In each case, the quality of the fine-tuning data determines how effectively the model adapts to its specialized role.

Training data is more than just a collection of information—it's what defines the strength, versatility, and limitations of AI systems. By grasping the intricacies of data selection, preparation, and application, you can better harness AI's potential, guiding it to generate more accurate, relevant, and insightful outputs. This understanding is fundamental for anyone working with AI, from developers to prompt engineers, and will be essential as we explore the power of these systems in real-world applications.

THE EVOLUTION OF AI: FROM RULE-BASED SYSTEMS TO GENERATIVE MODELS

Artificial intelligence has undergone a profound transformation over the decades, evolving from simple rule-based systems to the sophisticated generative models we see today. Understanding this progression is key to grasping the power of modern AI and its potential in the future.

In the early days of AI, systems were primarily rule-based. These systems, known as **expert systems,** followed explicit instructions or "if-then" rules to perform tasks. They relied on manually coded knowledge and could only handle well-defined, structured problems. For example, a rule-based system might help diagnose medical conditions by applying predefined rules that link symptoms to possible diseases. However, their limitations were clear: they couldn't learn from new data, adapt to unstructured inputs, or handle situations beyond the scope of their rules. The reliance on human-designed rules meant these systems lacked flexibility and scalability, often failing when faced with complexity or ambiguity.

As AI research progressed, researchers began exploring ways to make systems more adaptive and capable of learning from experience. This led to the rise of **machine learning** (ML), which shifted the focus from rigid programming to data-driven models. Unlike rule-based systems, ML models could adjust their behavior based on patterns in data, learning to make predictions or classifications without being explicitly programmed for every scenario. This was a crucial step forward, as it allowed AI to tackle more complex and varied tasks, such as recognizing images, understanding speech, or predicting future trends.

However, despite the success of machine learning, the next leap was a game changer: **generative models**. While traditional machine learning is primarily focused on making predictions based on input data, generative models go a step further. These models, such as Generative Adversarial Networks (GANs) and transformers like GPT, are designed to create new data—whether it's generating text, images, music, or even video. What sets generative models apart is their ability to produce content that seems original yet is based on patterns they've learned from vast datasets.

The breakthrough in generative models came with the introduction of **deep learning**, particularly **neural networks** that mimic the structure and functioning of the human brain. Deep learning models are capable of learning hierarchical representations of data, meaning they can analyze raw data (like pixels in an image or words in a sentence) and progressively extract more abstract features to generate coherent outputs. This approach allowed AI to excel at tasks such as natural language generation (NLG), where models like GPT-3 can craft entire paragraphs, articles, or even poetry with remarkable fluency.

What makes generative models so powerful is their ability to understand and generate complex patterns that are often too intricate for earlier rule-based or even traditional machine learning models. For example, GPT and similar models are trained on massive datasets, enabling them to generate human-like text that not only responds appropriately to prompts but also demonstrates creativity, coherence, and an understanding of context. They learn the structure of language—grammar, tone, intent—and can even produce outputs that exhibit subtle nuances like humor, emotion, or sarcasm.

However, this power comes with its own challenges. While rule-based systems had clear limits, the flexibility and complexity of generative models raise concerns about accuracy, bias, and ethical implications. For instance, while GPT can generate impressive results, it can also produce responses that are biased or factually incorrect, simply because it's trained on data that may contain such biases. Furthermore, the model's ability to generate highly convincing content poses questions around misinformation, security, and trust.

The evolution of AI—from rule-based systems to generative models—has radically transformed how we interact with machines. Today's systems offer incredible creativity, enabling them to produce outputs beyond prediction, like generating content that mirrors human thought. As these models continue to evolve, they promise even more powerful applications, but they also call for careful consideration of their impact on society, ethics, and the future of work.

CHAPTER 3: THE BASICS OF PROMPTS

Creating effective prompts is an art that requires a clear understanding of the task at hand and how to communicate it to an AI model. A good prompt is not just about being specific, but about offering the right context, structure, and tone. Throughout this chapter, we will explore the different types of prompts—ranging from simple requests to creative challenges—and dive into the most common mistakes people make when crafting them. By understanding the nuances of prompt writing, you'll be better equipped to guide AI in generating the results you want with precision and creativity.

WHAT MAKES A GOOD PROMPT?

Creating an effective prompt is at the heart of successful interaction with AI models. Whether you're using a large language model (LLM) like GPT for writing, answering questions, generating ideas, or any other task, the quality of the prompt you provide can drastically affect the output. But what makes a good prompt, and why does it matter?

A good prompt is clear, concise, and contextually rich. It sets the stage for the AI to understand what is being asked of it. To break this down further, let's look at the key elements that contribute to crafting a strong, effective prompt.

Clarity

The first and most important quality of a good prompt is clarity. If your instructions to the AI are vague, the AI will often return responses that are just as unclear. Ambiguity in the prompt leaves room for the model to misinterpret the task, leading to results that may not meet your expectations. For example, a prompt like *"Tell me something interesting"* is too open-ended and lacks clear direction. A better prompt might be *"Tell me an interesting fact about the history of the Internet"*. This tells the AI exactly what you're looking for, and it will have a much higher chance of providing you with relevant and focused information.

Being clear doesn't mean being overly simplistic, though. A good prompt also involves specifying the **scope** and **purpose**. For example, if you want the model to summarize an article, specify the length of the summary and whether you want to highlight specific sections or concepts.

Context

In addition to clarity, a good prompt provides enough context for the AI to understand the task. The more context you give, the more accurate and relevant the AI's response will be. For example, if you ask the AI to generate a marketing slogan for a new brand, it helps to provide additional information, such as the target audience, the product's unique features, or the tone of voice you want to convey. Without context, the AI might create a generic slogan that doesn't align with your needs.

Context also involves specifying the **desired format**. If you're requesting a step-by-step guide, make sure the prompt indicates

this. Similarly, if you need a formal or informal response, mentioning that can ensure the tone of the answer aligns with your expectations.

Specificity

Being specific in your prompts can guide the AI toward the type of answer you're seeking. When you ask a broad question, like *"Tell me about climate change"*, the response will likely cover a wide range of information. However, if you refine your prompt to something like *"Explain the impact of climate change on agriculture in the U.S."*, the AI will hone in on the more relevant data and provide you with a much more targeted answer.

This concept applies not just to questions but to other tasks, too. For instance, if you're asking for help with writing, you could specify things like word count, genre, or the style of writing you're aiming for. A prompt such as *"Write a 300-word blog post in a conversational tone about AI's role in healthcare"* gives the model clear boundaries and a precise goal.

4. Conciseness

While providing context and specificity is important, it's also essential not to overload the prompt with excessive detail. Too many instructions or unnecessary information can overwhelm the AI, causing it to focus on irrelevant aspects and produce a less focused answer. A good prompt strikes a balance between being detailed enough to provide guidance while being concise enough to avoid confusion.

Consider the difference between the following two prompts:

- *"Tell me about the effects of climate change, including how it affects weather patterns, sea levels, ecosystems, and human societies, and explain the science behind each one."*

- *"Explain the effects of climate change on ecosystems and human societies."*

The second prompt is more concise, guiding the AI to focus only on the two most important aspects without unnecessary elaboration.

Avoiding Ambiguity

Ambiguity is the enemy of effective prompts. AI models, especially those based on deep learning, often rely on the structure and patterns in language to predict the most likely response. When your prompt contains words or phrases that have multiple meanings or can be interpreted in several ways, the model might generate an answer that doesn't meet your needs. To avoid ambiguity, always aim for **precision**. For example, instead of asking *"What's the best way to train a model?"*, specify which kind of model you're referring to, whether it's a machine learning model, a language model, or another type.

Furthermore, be mindful of your word choices. Terms like "best," "good," or "interesting" are subjective. While the AI might understand these words, it cannot interpret them with the same nuance a human would. If you want specific insights, provide clear definitions or frameworks for what you consider "best" or "good." For instance, *"What is the most effective way to train a deep learning model for image recognition?"* provides clear parameters for the AI to work within.

6. Task Alignment

Finally, the prompt should be closely aligned with the task at hand. If you're looking for a creative solution, your prompt should reflect that need. If you're seeking factual data, the prompt should specify that as well. If you're asking the AI to write a piece of creative fiction, make sure the prompt directs the AI to that creative mode. Similarly, if you're requesting factual analysis, avoid elements that might cause the AI to produce speculative or fictional content.

Example Breakdown

Let's break down a sample prompt to see these principles in action. Suppose you're trying to generate a blog post about artificial intelligence in healthcare.

- **Poor Prompt**: *"Write about AI in healthcare."* This prompt is too vague, leaving the AI to determine the direction and scope of the response.

- **Better Prompt**: *"Write a 500-word blog post about how AI is transforming healthcare, focusing on patient diagnostics and drug discovery. Use a friendly, conversational tone, and include examples of current applications."* This prompt gives clear instructions on the length, focus, tone, and even the inclusion of real-world examples, setting the AI up for success.

What makes a good prompt is a combination of clarity, context, specificity, conciseness, and the elimination of ambiguity. A good prompt provides the AI with clear instructions on what is needed while offering enough context to guide its response. As you refine your skills in prompt engineering, these principles will become second nature, allowing you to consistently craft prompts that lead to high-quality, relevant, and focused AI-generated content.

TYPES OF PROMPTS: SIMPLE, INSTRUCTIONAL, CREATIVE

Understanding the different types of prompts is crucial when working with AI. Each type serves a specific purpose and can lead to different outputs, depending on how you approach your interaction. Let's break down three fundamental categories of prompts: simple, instructional, and creative.

Simple Prompts are the most basic form. These prompts are straightforward and usually consist of short, concise instructions or questions. For instance, a simple prompt might be "What's the capital of France?" or "Define AI." While these prompts are effective for getting direct answers or brief responses, they tend to be limited in the complexity of the output. AI can provide quick, factual answers based on its training data, but they often lack nuance or depth. Simple prompts are useful for quick facts, definitions, or basic queries.

Instructional Prompts go beyond simple requests and are used when you need the AI to perform a task or follow specific guidelines. These prompts often contain clear instructions about what you expect the model to do. An example might be, "Write a 200-word essay on climate change, focusing on the impact on coastal cities." Instructional prompts require the AI to not only understand the task at hand but also to adhere to specific requirements, such as word count, structure, or tone. These prompts are ideal when you need AI to generate something that fits within defined parameters or constraints.

Creative Prompts, on the other hand, are where AI can truly shine. These prompts are used when you want the AI to think outside the box, generate unique ideas, or engage in more complex creative tasks. For example, you might ask, "Write a short story set in a future where humans live on Mars" or "Generate five innovative business ideas for an AI startup." Creative prompts encourage the AI to take more liberties in its responses and allow for the generation of imaginative or original content. These prompts often require a more flexible approach, as the desired outcome may not be strictly defined. They allow the AI to explore different avenues of possibility, leading to a wide range of interesting and diverse outputs.

Each type of prompt has its place, and understanding when to use them will help you harness the full potential of AI. Simple prompts are great for getting quick, factual responses, instructional prompts are perfect for structured tasks, and creative prompts unlock AI's ability to think freely and generate innovative ideas.

COMMON MISTAKES WHEN WRITING PROMPTS

As with any skill, prompt engineering involves a learning curve, and even experienced users can make mistakes. By being aware of common pitfalls, you can refine your ability to interact effectively with AI models. Here are some common mistakes to avoid when crafting prompts:

1. Lack of Clarity and Precision

One of the most frequent mistakes is writing prompts that are vague or ambiguous. AI models, while powerful, rely on the input provided to generate responses. If your prompt is unclear, the AI may interpret it in unintended ways, leading to irrelevant or incomplete results. For instance, asking "Tell me about history" is too broad. The AI won't know which specific part of history you're interested in—whether it's a particular era, country, or event. To avoid this, make your prompts as specific as possible. Instead of "Tell me about history," try "Provide a brief overview of the Industrial Revolution in Europe."

2. Overcomplicating Prompts

While detail can be helpful, overwhelming the AI with too much information in a single prompt can have the opposite effect. Overloaded prompts may confuse the AI or lead to muddled responses. For example, asking, "Write a 500-word essay about the role of AI in modern education, including its impact on students, teachers, and educational institutions, and providing examples from different countries," could be too much to process in one go, especially if you need a more focused response. It's often better to break down complex tasks into smaller, manageable prompts, allowing the AI to focus on one aspect at a time.

3. Not Providing Enough Context

AI models perform best when they have context to work with. When a prompt lacks sufficient background or instructions, the response may feel disjointed or generic. For example, if you ask "Write a poem," the result might be technically correct but uninspired or unfocused. Instead, provide a framework: "Write a poem about autumn, using imagery of falling leaves and the change of seasons." Context helps guide the AI to produce more relevant and creative responses, aligning them with your expectations.

4. Assuming AI Understands Everything

While AI models are sophisticated, they don't have true comprehension or understanding of the world like humans do. They don't "know" things in the same way we do; they predict patterns based on their training data. It's important not to assume that AI can handle complex, nuanced requests without clear guidance. For instance, asking an AI to "generate a business plan" without specifying the industry or market could result in a vague or generic plan. Always provide context, background, and clear instructions when making requests.

5. Ignoring the Limitations of AI Models

AI models, despite their impressive abilities, still have limitations. They may struggle with understanding highly specialized language or intricate contexts, and they cannot produce real-time or up-to-date information. It's also important to note that AI models might generate content that is inaccurate, biased, or incomplete. Over-relying on AI for tasks that require high levels of expertise or nuanced judgment can lead to misleading results. Being aware of these limitations will help you set realistic expectations for the outcomes of your prompts.

6. Using Too Many Open-Ended Questions

Open-ended questions can be a great tool in certain contexts, but they can also result in overly broad or unspecific responses. For example, asking, "How does AI change the world?" is an incredibly vast question. It might lead the AI to generate a response that touches on various aspects, but without a clear direction or focus. Instead, narrow down your inquiry: "How does AI impact healthcare in developing countries?" A more focused prompt gives the AI a clearer direction, leading to more useful and actionable results.

7. Not Iterating or Refining Prompts

Sometimes, the first prompt you write might not yield the best results. It's important to view prompt engineering as an iterative process. If the AI's response isn't quite what you're looking for, refine your prompt and try again. Small adjustments—like rephrasing the question, adding more context, or specifying a tone—can significantly improve the outcome. Don't be afraid to experiment and adapt your approach based on the results you receive.

BUILDING EFFECTIVE PROMPTS

CHAPTER 4: THE ART OF CLARITY

Clarity is the cornerstone of effective prompt engineering. To get the best results from AI, you need to ensure that your prompts are structured clearly and free of ambiguity. In this chapter, we'll explore how to create precise, concise prompts that leave little room for misinterpretation. We'll also discuss how context can play a pivotal role in shaping the responses you receive, guiding AI to provide more relevant and accurate outputs. By mastering the art of clarity, you'll enhance your ability to communicate effectively with AI models and get the results you need.

STRUCTURING CLEAR AND CONCISE PROMPTS

When crafting prompts for AI models, structure plays a critical role in how effectively the AI can respond. A well-structured prompt ensures that the AI can process your request with minimal ambiguity and delivers results that are relevant and accurate.

Start by being specific. The more details you provide, the clearer the AI's understanding will be. Instead of asking vague questions like "Tell me about technology," opt for something more defined, such as "Explain the impact of artificial intelligence in healthcare." By narrowing down the focus, you provide the AI with a clearer direction to follow.

Next, aim for simplicity. While details are essential, overly complex or convoluted language can confuse the AI. Break your prompt into digestible parts, and avoid using unnecessary jargon or ambiguous phrases. For example, instead of saying, "Can you provide an in-depth explanation of the complex relationship between quantum computing and machine learning with a detailed analysis of the mathematical principles behind their interactions?" simplify it to: "Explain the connection between quantum computing and machine learning, highlighting the key concepts."

Another important aspect is to maintain a logical flow. Present your request in a manner that makes sense, both to you and to the AI. If you need the AI to perform multiple tasks or address different elements, structure your prompt in a step-by-step fashion. For example, you might start with an introductory statement or question, followed by clarifying instructions, and finish with a specific request or outcome you are expecting.

Finally, use appropriate framing. A concise question or directive that frames the context properly can make a world of difference. For instance, framing a prompt with "As an expert in climate science, explain..." signals to the AI the level of depth and tone expected in the response.

Clear and concise prompts allow the AI to focus on delivering the information or results you want, without getting bogged down in ambiguity. Remember that with clarity, less is often more: a simple, well-structured prompt can lead to more accurate and useful outputs.

AVOIDING AMBIGUITY AND VAGUENESS

Ambiguity and vagueness are the silent killers of effective prompts. When a prompt lacks clarity, it can lead to responses that are irrelevant, imprecise, or downright confusing. Therefore, avoiding ambiguity is a critical skill in prompt engineering.

One of the main reasons for ambiguity in prompts is the use of imprecise or broad language. For example, asking "Tell me about history" leaves too much room for interpretation. History is a vast subject that could span centuries and continents. What specific aspect of history do you want to know about? Are you interested in a specific period, event, or region? A more precise question like "What were the key factors leading to the fall of the Roman Empire?" will lead to a more focused and relevant response.

Similarly, vague wording often creates confusion for AI models. For instance, a prompt like "Explain technology" is too broad and doesn't provide enough direction. Instead, be specific about the type of technology you're referring to. Are you asking about the evolution of mobile phones, the rise of artificial intelligence, or blockchain? Providing context like "Explain how artificial intelligence is changing industries like healthcare and finance" narrows down the scope, guiding the AI to deliver a more accurate and detailed response.

Another common form of vagueness arises from the lack of clear instructions. A prompt like "Write a story" is open to interpretation. What genre? What tone? What kind of characters or plot are expected? By adding details like "Write a short mystery story set in a dystopian future" or "Create a motivational story featuring a young entrepreneur," you offer the AI a more structured approach, making it easier for the system to generate a response that aligns with your needs.

Another technique to avoid vagueness is ensuring that your requests are free from unnecessary jargon or overly complex phrasing. While you might be an expert in a specific field, your AI model might not be as familiar with specialized terms or industry-specific language. If you use unclear or overly technical terms without defining them, it can make the prompt difficult for the AI to understand. For instance, instead of using highly specific jargon like "Describe the implications of CRISPR-Cas9 in genetic engineering," you might first want to clarify the term: "Describe the implications of the CRISPR-Cas9 gene-editing tool in genetic engineering."

Finally, make sure to avoid contradictions within your prompt. A contradictory request can confuse both you and the AI. For example, "Write a romantic story about a couple who can never meet each other" could be interpreted in different ways. If you want to convey the idea of long-distance relationships or star-crossed lovers, it's better to clarify the scenario so the AI can generate a more coherent response.

The key to avoiding ambiguity and vagueness is to ask specific, clear questions that direct the AI's attention to what matters most. By being intentional with your wording and structuring your prompts carefully, you reduce the chances of miscommunication and increase the likelihood of receiving meaningful and accurate results.

USING CONTEXT TO ENHANCE RESPONSES

Context is one of the most powerful tools at your disposal when crafting prompts. Without it, AI models often struggle to generate responses that truly match your expectations. By adding the right context to your prompts, you give the AI the necessary background to tailor its responses in a way that is not only relevant but also aligned with your specific needs.

When we talk about "context" in prompt engineering, we mean the relevant information surrounding the subject of your query. This could include historical background, the current scenario, a specific audience, or any additional details that narrow down the focus. Context helps guide the AI's processing, enabling it to understand your intent more clearly and produce responses that are specific, coherent, and useful.

Consider a simple question like, "What are the health benefits of exercise?" On its own, this prompt could lead to a general list of benefits. However, if you add context by specifying the type of exercise you're referring to—such as "What are the health benefits of cardiovascular exercise for elderly individuals?"—the AI can offer a response that is tailored to that particular demographic, focusing on relevant concerns like heart health, mobility, and fitness in older adults.

Similarly, context can be used to refine the tone or style of the response. Let's say you want a summary of a scientific article. You might be asking the AI to create a concise version of a complex text, but the way you frame that request can make a difference. By adding context like, "Summarize the article in a way that's easy for a general audience to understand," you guide the AI to adjust its language and structure, ensuring that the summary isn't laden with technical jargon, but instead accessible and comprehensible.

Another effective way to use context is by including examples. If you're looking for help writing a poem, a basic prompt like "Write a poem about nature" could result in a wide range of outputs, some of which may not resonate with your intentions. However, if you provide additional context like "Write a poem about a mountain landscape in the style of Robert Frost," the AI will have a clearer sense of your expectations and style, leading to a more accurate response.

In some cases, especially when working with larger and more complex models, it's also helpful to provide a little bit of context about the model's limitations or scope. For example, if you're generating a piece of creative writing, and you want it to avoid certain clichés, you can specify, "Write a love story without using common phrases like 'heart skips a beat' or 'you complete me.'" This additional context helps prevent the AI from falling back on overused expressions and makes the final result more unique.

The key to using context effectively is balance. Too little context leaves the AI with too much room for interpretation, leading to generic or irrelevant responses. Too much context, on the other hand, can overwhelm the model or narrow its focus too much, possibly leaving out important aspects of your query. Strive for clarity and specificity, providing just enough context for the AI to produce the results you expect.

In summary, context acts as a guide for the AI, ensuring that its responses align more closely with your needs. By embedding the right level of context in your prompts, you not only improve the relevance of the generated output but also enhance the overall efficiency and quality of your AI interactions.

CHAPTER 5: PROMPT STRATEGIES

Effective prompt engineering goes beyond just asking questions—it's about choosing the right strategy for the task at hand. In this chapter, we'll explore different types of prompt strategies, from open-ended prompts that encourage creativity and expansive thinking, to closed-ended prompts that drive specific, actionable responses. We'll also dive into the power of multi-step prompts for handling more complex tasks and how using examples can help guide AI's behavior more precisely. Mastering these strategies will not only help you get the answers you need but also ensure that those answers are tailored to your specific goals.

OPEN-ENDED VS. CLOSED-ENDED PROMPTS

When crafting prompts, one of the first decisions you'll make is whether to use an open-ended or closed-ended approach. This distinction is fundamental because it directly influences the type and depth of response you receive from AI.

Open-ended prompts encourage exploration, inviting the AI to generate broader, more creative, and expansive answers. For example, asking "What are some ways AI can impact healthcare?" allows the model to delve into a wide range of possibilities, from technological advancements to ethical considerations. Open-ended prompts are ideal when you're seeking detailed, diverse insights or creative solutions. They can lead to innovative ideas, but they also require you to manage the resulting complexity.

On the other hand, **closed-ended prompts** are more specific, usually leading to shorter, more focused answers. These prompts work well when you need precise, factual information or a yes/no response. For instance, asking "Is AI used in diagnostics?" will elicit a direct answer. While closed-ended prompts limit the response scope, they can be invaluable when time is tight or when you need clarity and precision.

Both types of prompts have their place depending on the task at hand. Open-ended prompts allow for a deeper exploration of a topic, while closed-ended prompts can save time and provide concrete answers. Mastering when to use each type, and how to balance them, will enhance your ability to extract the most relevant and useful information from AI, depending on your needs.

MULTI-STEP PROMPTS FOR COMPLEX TASKS

When dealing with complex tasks, **multi-step prompts** can be incredibly useful. These prompts break down a larger, more intricate task into manageable, sequential steps, guiding the AI through the process in a structured way. By doing so, you can ensure the AI's responses are more coherent and aligned with your goals.

Consider the scenario where you need AI to assist in writing an in-depth article on a technical subject. A single, broad prompt may not yield the desired result because the AI could struggle with the complexity or miss essential components. Instead, breaking the task into smaller steps can significantly improve the output.

For instance, you could begin by prompting the AI with a question like, "Can you list the main concepts related to [subject]?" Once you have a list, you could follow up with, "Now, explain each concept briefly." Next, ask the AI to "Provide an example for each concept." Finally, conclude with, "Summarize how these concepts are interrelated." Each step allows the AI to focus on a specific aspect of the task, reducing the likelihood of errors or confusion.

Multi-step prompts help the AI to follow a logical flow, producing responses that build upon each other. This method is particularly effective when you're dealing with complex ideas or processes that require detailed, thoughtful responses. It's a great way to maintain clarity and structure, ensuring that the AI delivers consistent, relevant information.

By breaking tasks into digestible chunks, you help the AI process the information in a way that reflects your own approach to tackling problems.

USING EXAMPLES TO GUIDE AI BEHAVIOR

Examples serve as a concrete illustration of the behavior or response you want from the AI. Instead of just asking a vague question, you can show the AI exactly how to respond, which helps it grasp the nuances of your request. By embedding examples into your prompts, you can shape the AI's responses to fit a specific tone, structure, or level of detail.

How Examples Shape Responses

Let's look at a few scenarios to see how examples can guide AI behavior:

1. **Defining Tone and Style:** Imagine you want the AI to generate a response in a formal tone. Rather than simply stating, "Write in a formal tone," you can provide an example of the type of language you're expecting. For example, you might say:

   ○ *"Please write the following paragraph in a formal tone, like this example: 'In conclusion, the findings of the research suggest that a robust approach is necessary for addressing the challenges at hand. Further analysis is required to fully understand the implications.' Now, write about the importance of education in society using a similar formal tone."*

By providing an example, you're not only specifying the tone but also giving the AI a model to follow, reducing the risk of an overly casual or inappropriate response.

2. **Clarifying Content Structure:** Examples can also be useful for guiding the structure of the response. Suppose you want a detailed answer on a specific topic, and you want to ensure the AI provides an introduction, followed by arguments, and a conclusion. You can prompt it like this:

   ○ *"Please respond to the following question in the format of an essay with an introduction, body paragraphs, and a conclusion: 'What are the benefits of renewable energy?' Here's an example of how I want the structure to look: 'Introduction:*

Renewable energy is becoming more important in today's world due to environmental concerns. Body: The benefits of renewable energy include reducing greenhouse gas emissions, lowering energy costs, and providing sustainable power sources. Conclusion: In conclusion, renewable energy offers long-term advantages for both the environment and the economy.'"

This clear structural guidance helps the AI understand exactly how to organize its response, which can be particularly helpful for complex topics.

3. **Demonstrating Specific Responses:** Sometimes, you might want the AI to respond in a very specific way, like summarizing information or listing key points. To guide the AI, you can show it a previous example. For instance:

   o *"Summarize the following article in three points, like this example: '1. The importance of urban gardening for sustainability. 2. How cities can benefit from green spaces. 3. The challenges of implementing urban gardening projects.' Now, summarize the article about the impacts of climate change on agriculture in three points."*

In this case, the AI knows exactly what type of summary you're expecting—concise, bullet-pointed, and focused on key aspects.

4. **Setting Constraints or Limitations:** You might also want to set some constraints or limits on the response. For example, if you're asking the AI to generate a creative piece, you might want to make sure it doesn't go too far

out of bounds. You can use examples to show what's acceptable:

> o   *"Write a short story in a science-fiction setting, but keep it under 200 words and avoid any complex scientific jargon, like in this example: 'A future where robots control the weather and humans are forced to adapt. The protagonist, an engineer, finds a way to communicate with the machines and changes the climate for the better.' Now, write your own story about a future society where technology controls transportation."*

By providing both the context and constraints, you're helping the AI stay within the desired parameters, ensuring it doesn't deviate from your vision.

5. **Clarifying Complex Ideas:** If you're working with a topic that might be difficult for the AI to understand or if you want a specific type of explanation, providing an example is a great way to ensure clarity. For example, if you're asking the AI to explain a technical concept in simple terms, you can guide it like this:

> o   *"Explain the concept of quantum mechanics as if you were explaining it to a 10-year-old, like this example: 'Quantum mechanics is like a game where tiny particles can be in many places at once. Imagine you have a magic coin that can land on heads and tails at the same time.' Now, explain the concept of artificial intelligence in simple terms."*

Here, you provide a model explanation that helps the AI understand the level of simplicity and the approach you want it to use.

Examples in Action: The Power of Clear Guidance

Let's put everything together with a few examples showing how powerful well-crafted prompts with examples can be:

- **Example 1:**

  - *"Generate a list of reasons why exercise is beneficial for health, like this example: '1. Improves cardiovascular health. 2. Boosts mental clarity and reduces stress. 3. Enhances muscle strength and endurance. 4. Promotes better sleep. 5. Reduces the risk of chronic diseases.' Now, list the benefits of eating a balanced diet."*

- **Example 2:**

  - *"Write a review of a movie you've watched, using the structure of this example: 'Title: Inception. Review: Inception is a mind-bending film that explores the concept of dreams within dreams. The direction by Christopher Nolan is top-notch, and the performances are stellar. However, the complex plot may be difficult for some viewers to follow. Overall, it's a must-see for fans of psychological thrillers.' Now, write a review of 'The Matrix'."*

In both examples, the AI is provided with a clear structure and the kind of information you're looking for, improving the chances of it producing accurate and relevant content.

Why This Approach Works

Using examples works because it aligns the AI's responses with your expectations, reducing the risk of misinterpretation. It also allows the AI to tap into patterns it's already learned, leading to more accurate and creative outputs. In essence, examples give the AI a template to follow, which enhances the overall quality of the response.

By showing the AI how to respond rather than just telling it, you create a more intuitive interaction. The examples essentially act as a bridge between your request and the AI's processing abilities, ensuring that the end result is what you were hoping for.

In summary, when writing prompts, don't hesitate to provide clear, concise examples that illustrate the kind of response you're looking for. This method not only helps the AI understand the task but also fine-tunes its output, bringing you closer to achieving your goals.

CHAPTER 6: ADVANCED TECHNIQUES

As you become more comfortable with prompt engineering, it's time to explore some advanced techniques that can unlock even greater potential from AI models. In this chapter, we'll look at how fine-tuning your prompts can lead to more precise and tailored outputs. We'll also dive into system messages—how adjusting settings like temperature and providing role instructions can significantly influence AI behavior. Additionally, we'll explore chaining prompts, a technique that allows for dynamic interactions and evolving conversations.

FINE-TUNING PROMPTS FOR SPECIFIC OUTPUTS

Fine-tuning a prompt doesn't mean changing the core idea of your request; it's about modifying how you express that request to steer the AI toward a specific type of response. The key to fine-tuning lies in the balance between providing enough detail to guide the AI and leaving enough flexibility for creativity. Too little detail may result in vague or irrelevant responses, while too much detail can limit the AI's creativity and lead to overly rigid outputs.

The process involves three main steps:

1. **Clarifying the Output Type**: Define what kind of output you want. Are you asking for a list, a detailed explanation, a short summary, or a creative piece? The clearer you are, the more the AI can focus on the right style and format.

2. **Incorporating Specific Details**: Include necessary information that will direct the AI to tailor its response. This might involve adding constraints (e.g., word count), context (e.g., previous information), or tone (e.g., formal, casual).

3. **Testing and Iteration**: Fine-tuning is an iterative process. You might need to adjust your prompt a few times to get the response that matches your expectations. Think of this as a back-and-forth dialogue with the AI, where you progressively refine the prompt for better results.

Examples of Fine-Tuning Prompts for Specific Outputs

Let's explore how fine-tuning works in practice with detailed examples. These scenarios will show you how you can adjust prompts to get a more targeted output.

1. Fine-Tuning for Creative Writing

Suppose you want the AI to write a short story, but you have a very specific genre, theme, and character in mind. A general prompt like "Write a short story" may give you a broad, unfocused result. However, by fine-tuning the prompt, you can guide the AI toward your ideal outcome.

General Prompt:

- *"Write a short story."*

Fine-Tuned Prompt:

- *"Write a 500-word science fiction short story set in a dystopian future where robots have taken over the world. The protagonist, a young rebel, must confront a robot overlord to save humanity. Make the tone serious and suspenseful, and include a twist at the end."*

This fine-tuned prompt provides more details about the genre, plot, tone, and word count, which leads to a much more focused and relevant response. It's clear what type of story the AI should generate, including the mood and structure.

2. Fine-Tuning for Technical Explanations

Imagine you need the AI to explain a complex technical concept, but you want the explanation to be simple enough for a beginner to understand. A general prompt asking the AI to explain the concept may result in a response that's too detailed or technical for your audience. By fine-tuning the prompt, you can ensure the explanation is tailored to the right level of understanding.

General Prompt:

- *"Explain quantum computing."*

Fine-Tuned Prompt:

- *"Explain quantum computing in simple terms, as if you were teaching a high school student who has basic knowledge of computer science but is new to quantum mechanics. Include an analogy to help explain how quantum computers work."*

This refined prompt makes it clear that the explanation should be accessible to a high school student, and it asks for an analogy to simplify the concept further. This ensures that the AI doesn't dive too deep into technical jargon or overly complex explanations.

3. Fine-Tuning for Creative Content (e.g., Marketing Copy)

If you're asking the AI to generate content for marketing or advertising, it's essential to fine-tune the prompt to ensure the tone and language match your brand or campaign. A vague prompt might lead to generic content, while a fine-tuned prompt will align the output with your specific goals.

General Prompt:

- *"Write a product description."*

Fine-Tuned Prompt:

- *"Write a persuasive product description for a new high-end smartwatch aimed at tech-savvy professionals. The description should highlight the smartwatch's unique features like its long battery life, sleek design, and health-tracking capabilities. Use a confident and sophisticated tone that appeals to a premium audience."*

This fine-tuned prompt guides the AI to focus on specific features, target the right audience, and use the desired tone, ensuring the generated content aligns with your brand identity.

4. Fine-Tuning for Analytical Responses

In some cases, you may need the AI to analyze a situation or provide a structured answer to a complex question. Fine-tuning the prompt to focus on the specific type of analysis you want is crucial.

General Prompt:

- *"Analyze the economic impact of the COVID-19 pandemic."*

Fine-Tuned Prompt:

- *"Analyze the economic impact of the COVID-19 pandemic on small businesses in the United States. Provide a summary of the challenges faced, the role of government stimulus programs, and the long-term effects on local economies. Use data from 2020-2021 to support your analysis and organize the response in a clear, structured format."*

This prompt narrows down the scope of the analysis, specifying the region, target audience (small businesses), time frame, and required structure. The AI will now be better equipped to deliver an answer that's tailored to the specific focus you've requested.

The Importance of Iteration and Feedback

Even with the most carefully fine-tuned prompts, you may not always get the perfect result on the first try. Fine-tuning prompts is an iterative process, and it often involves trial and error. After receiving the AI's response, you might realize that you need to refine your instructions further or adjust some of the parameters.

For example, if the first response doesn't quite meet your expectations, you can tweak the prompt to clarify specific details or adjust the tone. Providing feedback to the AI helps refine the output over time, resulting in more precise and relevant answers. It's essential to keep experimenting and tweaking until the results match your exact needs.

Fine-Tuning for Specific Outputs: The Takeaway

In summary, **fine-tuning prompts** allows you to gain more control over the output, ensuring that the AI delivers exactly what you need. Whether you're looking for creative writing, technical explanations, analytical responses, or marketing copy, fine-tuning helps you craft prompts that are specific, clear, and focused. By understanding the importance of structure, context, and detail, you can guide the AI to produce high-quality, tailored outputs that align with your goals.

This process requires practice and careful attention to detail, but with time, it will enable you to leverage the full potential of AI and prompt engineering. So, as you move forward, remember that fine-tuning is not just about refining the words in your prompt but also about refining your understanding of what you want and how to communicate that to the AI.

LEVERAGING SYSTEM MESSAGES (TEMPERATURE, ROLE INSTRUCTIONS)

In AI prompt engineering, system messages—such as **temperature** and **role instructions**—play an essential role in shaping how the model generates responses. Understanding how to leverage these system parameters effectively can give you far more control over the AI's behavior, allowing you to tailor its output to match your specific needs.

What are System Messages?

System messages are internal configurations that influence the way an AI model behaves when responding to prompts. These messages are often not part of the direct input that you provide but instead act as invisible instructions that help guide the AI's response. They allow you to tweak aspects of the AI's personality, creativity, tone, and overall response style without directly modifying the prompt itself.

Among the most commonly used system messages are **temperature** and **role instructions**. These two parameters are powerful tools for controlling the kind of output the AI will produce, whether you're seeking highly creative responses, formal tone, or even more structured or factual outputs.

1. Temperature: Controlling Creativity and Variability

The **temperature** setting is one of the most crucial tools for adjusting the creativity and variability of an AI's responses. It essentially controls how much randomness or creativity is introduced into the AI's output. The higher the temperature, the more creative and varied the output will be, while a lower temperature produces more deterministic and conservative responses.

How Does Temperature Work?

Temperature is usually set on a scale from 0 to 1, with:

- **Low temperature (e.g., 0.2 - 0.3):** The output is more focused, consistent, and deterministic. It tends to stick closely to common patterns and provides safer, more predictable responses.

- **Medium temperature (e.g., 0.5 - 0.7):** This is a balanced setting, offering a mix of creativity and control. It's great when you want the AI to generate responses that are both coherent and slightly inventive, without going too far off course.

- **High temperature (e.g., 0.8 - 1.0):** The output becomes more diverse and imaginative, with greater potential for unique, out-of-the-box thinking. This setting can lead to responses that are less predictable and more creative, ideal for tasks like brainstorming, story generation, or generating novel ideas.

Example of Temperature in Action

Let's say you want the AI to generate a description of a futuristic city. Here's how the temperature would affect the output:

- **Low Temperature (0.2):**
    - *"The city is a modern metropolis with skyscrapers, well-maintained streets, and advanced public transport systems. It has a clean, efficient layout with a strong emphasis on sustainability."*

- **Medium Temperature (0.5):**

- *"The city towers into the sky, with reflective glass buildings that shimmer in the daylight. Streets are lined with green spaces, and autonomous vehicles glide silently through the city's efficient network. This is a place where technology and nature coexist in perfect harmony."*

- **High Temperature (0.9):**

  - *"A city built upon floating platforms, where buildings spiral like organic vines reaching for the clouds. Neon lights flicker along waterways that run through the streets, while aerial vehicles zoom overhead, leaving trails of iridescent vapor. It's a world where time bends, and the future is both chaotic and harmonious."*

As you can see, adjusting the temperature setting has a profound impact on the imagination and unpredictability of the output. Low temperatures generate more structured and conventional responses, while higher temperatures bring about creativity and unexpected ideas.

When to Use Different Temperature Settings

- **Low temperature:** Use this when you need clear, factual, or straightforward information. It's particularly useful for tasks like summarizing content, writing technical articles, or generating responses that require high precision.

- **Medium temperature:** This is ideal for tasks that require some level of creativity but still need to maintain coherence, such as writing blog posts, casual conversations, or generating ideas that are on-topic but innovative.

- **High temperature:** Perfect for brainstorming, creative writing, and generating diverse, out-of-the-box ideas. If you're looking to experiment with different perspectives or generate highly original content, this is the setting to use.

2. Role Instructions: Directing the AI's Persona and Behavior

Another critical system message is **role instructions**. These instructions essentially set the persona, tone, and approach the AI should adopt when generating responses. By providing explicit guidance about the AI's role, you can fine-tune its output in ways that are not immediately achievable with the prompt alone.

What Are Role Instructions?

Role instructions are used to define how the AI should behave in a specific context. This could involve guiding the AI to take on a particular persona, adopt a certain tone, or approach a problem from a specific angle. These instructions help align the AI's responses with your expectations by establishing a framework for how it should think, talk, or respond.

For example, you could specify that the AI should behave as if it's an expert in a field, a casual conversation partner, or even a customer support representative. The more detailed the role instructions, the more accurate and tailored the AI's response will be.

Examples of Role Instructions

1. **Casual Conversation Partner:**
    - *"You are a friendly, casual conversation partner who enjoys discussing hobbies, interests, and*

personal experiences. Keep the tone light, engaging, and approachable."

2. **Technical Expert:**

   o *"You are a computer science professor with years of experience in machine learning. Your explanations should be precise and clear, using examples to explain complex concepts in a simple way."*

3. **Customer Support Agent:**

   o *"You are a customer support representative for a tech company. Your responses should be empathetic, polite, and professional, with a focus on solving the customer's issue efficiently."*

Role Instructions in Practice

Let's consider the role instructions in action with an example. Suppose you want the AI to provide technical support for an issue related to a smartphone.

- **Without Role Instruction:**

  o *"How can I fix my phone when it's not charging?"*

  o The AI might respond with general instructions or possible causes of the issue without a clear tone or structure.

- **With Role Instruction (Customer Support):**

  o *"You are a customer support representative for a smartphone company. A customer is having trouble with their phone not charging. Be empathetic and provide step-by-step instructions to diagnose the issue."*

- o The AI might respond like this:
    - ▪ "I'm sorry to hear that your phone isn't charging! Let's try a few things to resolve the issue. First, please check if the charging cable is properly plugged into both the phone and the charger. If that's fine, try using a different charger to rule out a faulty cable. If the issue persists, there may be an issue with the phone's charging port, and I recommend bringing it to a service center for a closer inspection."

This demonstrates how role instructions help guide the AI's tone, professionalism, and level of detail.

Combining Temperature and Role Instructions

In many cases, you'll want to use both **temperature** and **role instructions** in tandem to create even more precise results. For example, if you want the AI to play the role of a teacher explaining a complicated concept, you could use both a moderate temperature for creativity and role instructions to define its teaching style.

Example:

- **Role Instruction**: *"You are a patient and detailed teacher explaining the concept of quantum mechanics to a group of university students. Use clear analogies and examples to make the material easy to understand."*

- **Temperature**: *0.6*

- **Resulting Output:**
  - *"Imagine you're walking through a park and see a ball rolling down the hill. Normally, you would expect the ball to follow a clear path. In the quantum world, though, the ball doesn't follow just one path. It exists in a superposition of many paths at the same time, only deciding on a single path when we observe it. This behavior is similar to what's called 'wave-particle duality.'"*

By carefully leveraging **system messages** such as **temperature** and **role instructions**, you can gain much more control over the AI's behavior and ensure that it delivers responses that match your specific needs. These settings enable you to adjust the level of creativity, detail, and tone, and provide further context to guide the AI's responses in the right direction. Whether you're seeking highly creative content or precise, professional responses, understanding how to fine-tune these system messages is crucial in AI prompt engineering.

CHAINING PROMPTS FOR DYNAMIC INTERACTIONS

When engaging with an AI, the ability to chain prompts together effectively allows for more dynamic, contextually aware, and coherent interactions. This technique enables you to build a conversation or task incrementally, creating a continuous flow of thought that mimics how humans communicate and think. By chaining prompts, you can ensure the AI responds with increasing complexity and depth, making it an invaluable tool for handling multi-step tasks or open-ended discussions.

What is Prompt Chaining?

Prompt chaining involves linking multiple prompts together in a sequence, where the output of one prompt serves as the input or context for the next. This process allows you to gradually build up the AI's understanding of a topic, guide its thought process over multiple steps, and refine the information as you go. Each prompt leads logically into the next, helping to maintain a consistent thread of logic and relevance across the interaction.

Think of it as a conversation where each exchange builds upon the previous one. For instance, you wouldn't expect a person to give you a perfect answer on their first try—often, you need to ask follow-up questions, clarify details, or narrow the focus. In the same way, chaining prompts lets you refine the AI's responses, guiding it through complex topics in manageable steps.

Why is Prompt Chaining Important?

The beauty of prompt chaining is that it allows for the creation of more sophisticated interactions with the AI. Rather than just relying on a single prompt to get a comprehensive answer, you can guide the AI through multiple phases, each tailored to a specific goal. This results in more nuanced, detailed, and accurate outputs, especially when dealing with complex topics, creative tasks, or long-form content creation.

Without chaining prompts, the AI may fail to fully grasp the context of a conversation, provide incomplete answers, or misunderstand the nuances of your request. Chaining allows you to overcome these limitations by giving the AI a chance to revise, reflect, and expand on its initial responses.

How to Chain Prompts Effectively

1. **Establish the Core Goal**: Before chaining prompts, define the overall goal of your interaction. Are you trying to write a detailed report? Solve a complex problem? Or generate creative content? Understanding your end objective will help you structure the prompts in a logical sequence.

Example Goal: Write a detailed article about the impact of AI in healthcare.

You wouldn't start by asking the AI for a fully written article right away. Instead, break the task into smaller components. Start by asking about the key points you want to address, followed by deeper questions about each individual aspect.

2. **Break Down Complex Tasks**: Divide your overarching task into manageable sub-tasks. These sub-tasks could be individual questions or smaller objectives that build toward the final result. Each step should refine the previous one, helping to clarify the AI's understanding.

Example Breakdown:

- **Step 1**: *"What are the key ways AI is currently being used in healthcare?"*

- **Step 2**: *"How does AI improve diagnostics in healthcare?"*

- **Step 3**: *"What challenges are associated with integrating AI into healthcare systems?"*

- Step 4: *"Summarize the benefits and challenges of AI in healthcare and suggest ways to overcome them."*

Here, you're gradually building up knowledge before synthesizing it into a cohesive output. Each prompt should refine the AI's understanding based on the previous interaction.

3. **Provide Context**: When chaining prompts, context becomes critical. The AI should retain the key information from previous steps to ensure coherence. One way to do this is by including a recap or summary of previous interactions, which helps maintain continuity and clarity.

Example Chained Prompts:

- **Prompt 1**: *"Explain the concept of machine learning."*

- **Prompt 2**: *"Now, given that machine learning involves large datasets, how can AI systems manage and process vast amounts of medical data?"*

- **Prompt 3**: *"Incorporating the idea of data processing from the last prompt, describe how AI can be used in predictive healthcare analytics."*

Notice that each subsequent prompt is informed by the previous one. By the time you get to Prompt 3, the AI should already understand the context of machine learning and its role in healthcare data.

4. **Refine Responses**: As you chain prompts, you can use each response as a stepping stone to refine and enhance the next one. Don't hesitate to ask follow-up questions or seek clarifications to ensure the AI's output matches

your desired level of depth and accuracy. The AI's first response might not always be perfect, and prompt chaining gives you the opportunity to guide it toward the ideal result.

Example: After receiving a response about AI in healthcare, you might ask:

- *"Can you expand more on the ethical concerns you mentioned?"* or

- *"Can you provide examples of successful AI applications in this field?"*

These additional prompts refine the AI's response, making it more specific and well-rounded.

5. **Use Clear Transitions Between Prompts**: The flow of ideas should feel natural, with each new prompt smoothly leading to the next. Clear transitions between prompts help the AI understand the sequence of tasks and how each part fits into the larger picture.

Example Transition:

- **Prompt 1**: *"What are the latest trends in artificial intelligence?"*

- **Prompt 2**: *"How do these trends affect the business landscape?"*

- **Prompt 3**: *"Given these trends and their effects on business, how can companies strategically implement AI to drive growth?"*

In this chain, the questions are interconnected and logically follow from one another. The AI can follow this progression to create a coherent answer.

6. **Consider Using Output from One Prompt as Input for Another**: One of the most effective ways to chain prompts is by using the output of one prompt directly as input for another. This approach allows you to guide the conversation and focus on specific aspects that are most relevant to your task.

Example: If you're writing a creative story:

- **Prompt 1**: *"Generate a list of potential character traits for a superhero."*

- **Prompt 2**: *"Using the traits from the previous list, develop the backstory of a character with those traits."*

- **Prompt 3**: *"How does this character evolve throughout the story?"*

The output from each step feeds directly into the next, helping you build a well-rounded character from multiple angles.

Benefits of Chaining Prompts

- **Improved Coherence and Consistency**: Chaining prompts ensures that the AI doesn't lose track of the conversation or task. By keeping the context intact, you can make sure the AI's output remains coherent, even across multiple steps.

- **Increased Flexibility**: Chaining allows you to pivot or adjust the task as you go. If you realize that one aspect of the topic needs further exploration, you can easily add new prompts to dive deeper without starting from scratch.

- **More Detailed and Tailored Responses**: Each prompt in the chain can focus on a specific sub-topic, allowing the AI to go deeper into the subject matter. This results in responses that are more detailed and personalized to your exact needs.

- **Better Control Over the Output**: With prompt chaining, you maintain control over how the AI's response develops. This is especially important for tasks that require a structured approach, like reports, articles, or creative writing.

Example Use Case: Problem-Solving

Imagine you're working on a problem-solving task, such as optimizing the performance of a machine learning model. Chaining prompts can help you break the problem down into smaller, manageable chunks.

- **Step 1**: *"What are the key factors that affect the performance of a machine learning model?"*

- **Step 2**: *"Based on the factors identified, how can you optimize data preprocessing to improve model performance?"*

- **Step 3**: *"What machine learning algorithms are best suited for improving accuracy in predictive models?"*

- **Step 4**: *"How can model evaluation metrics be used to assess the success of optimizations?"*

By chaining these prompts together, you can guide the AI through the entire problem-solving process, from identifying the key factors to evaluating the success of your solution.

Chaining prompts is a powerful technique that allows you to have dynamic, structured interactions with AI. By linking multiple prompts together in a logical sequence, you can guide the AI through complex tasks, build up knowledge incrementally, and refine its outputs step by step. This process enables you to maintain continuity, coherence, and control over the AI's responses, making it an invaluable tool in AI prompt engineering. Whether you're solving problems, conducting research, or crafting creative content, prompt chaining ensures that the AI delivers high-quality results every time.

USE CASES AND APPLICATIONS

CHAPTER 7: PROMPT ENGINEERING FOR PROFESSIONALS

Prompt engineering has become an indispensable tool for professionals across industries, enabling efficiency, creativity, and precision in daily tasks. This chapter delves into how prompts can revolutionize content creation, from drafting blogs and marketing copy to scripting videos. For researchers, AI becomes a valuable assistant, summarizing complex information, generating fresh ideas, and performing in-depth analyses. Developers, too, can benefit, using AI to debug code, provide solutions, and even generate new programming ideas. By tailoring your prompts to specific professional needs, you'll not only save time but also enhance the quality of your outputs, opening doors to new levels of productivity.

CONTENT CREATION (BLOGS, MARKETING, SCRIPTS)

In the world of content creation, whether it's blogs, marketing materials, or scripts, the role of AI has grown exponentially. The beauty of prompt engineering lies in its ability to assist in shaping and enhancing content by producing highly tailored responses that fit your needs, whether you're writing for a blog, crafting persuasive marketing copy, or generating engaging scripts.

Let's start with blogs. Writing a blog post can be a daunting task, but with the right prompts, AI can help you brainstorm, structure, and even draft sections of the post. The key is to provide context within the prompt—be specific about the audience, the style of writing, and the core message you want to convey. For example, if you're writing a blog post about AI advancements, a prompt like "Write a 600-word blog post about the impact of AI in healthcare for a general audience, using a friendly, approachable tone" will lead to an AI-generated response that aligns with your expectations. With the right input, you can drastically reduce the time spent on research and drafting.

Marketing, on the other hand, requires a different approach. It's not just about content; it's about persuasion and driving action. AI-driven prompts here need to be focused on creating compelling, action-oriented language. Whether you're writing copy for an ad, an email campaign, or landing pages, the power of AI can be harnessed to craft attention-grabbing headlines, emotional appeals, and value propositions. Prompts like "Generate three different versions of a Facebook ad copy for a new fitness app targeting women aged 25-40, emphasizing health and convenience" will produce copy that's customized to your goals and audience.

For scripts—whether for videos, podcasts, or presentations—the key challenge is maintaining flow while keeping the content engaging. AI can help here too by generating conversational dialogues, offering transitions, and even suggesting ways to introduce complex topics in simple, relatable terms. For example, if you need a script for a corporate video, a prompt like "Create a 2-minute script introducing a new product in a way that's informative but also entertaining for a tech-savvy audience" will give you a starting point that can be refined to fit your voice and style.

Ultimately, effective prompt engineering for content creation is about clarity, specificity, and intention. The more defined your prompt, the better the AI output will be. But it's not just about having AI do the heavy lifting—it's about collaborating with AI to enhance your creative process, streamline workflows, and push the boundaries of what you can accomplish.

RESEARCH ASSISTANCE (SUMMARIZATION, ANALYSIS, IDEA GENERATION)

In the age of information overload, the need for effective research assistance has never been more important. AI-driven tools, particularly through prompt engineering, can help you sift through vast amounts of data, providing clear, concise summaries, deeper analysis, and even sparking fresh ideas. Whether you're working on an academic project, business research, or simply exploring a new topic, the right prompts can significantly enhance your research process, making it faster and more efficient.

Let's begin with **summarization**. One of the most valuable applications of AI in research is its ability to digest long articles, reports, or papers and condense them into digestible, key points. Instead of manually reading through pages of information, you can craft a prompt that instructs the AI to extract the most important insights. For example, you might use a prompt like, "Summarize the key points of this 10-page research paper on climate change, focusing on the findings and conclusions." This will allow you to quickly grasp the essence of the document without losing the nuances. For even more tailored results, you can request specific details to be emphasized in the summary, such as methodology, case studies, or data trends.

Next, there's **analysis**. Research often requires deep understanding and interpretation of complex data or concepts. AI can be invaluable here by helping you break down intricate information, drawing connections, and offering insightful interpretations. For instance, if you're working with a dataset or a theoretical concept, you could ask the AI, "Analyze the relationship between increasing urbanization and climate change in developing countries based on this dataset," and it will offer an interpretation of the data, highlighting trends, correlations, and potential implications. AI's ability to process large volumes of information in seconds, combined with prompt engineering, allows you to focus more on interpreting results rather than spending excessive time sifting through raw data.

Idea generation is another crucial aspect of research where prompt engineering can make a huge difference. Whether you're brainstorming new topics, formulating hypotheses, or looking for creative solutions, AI can serve as a powerful tool for expanding your thought process. A well-crafted prompt can guide the AI to produce a variety of suggestions that align with your interests and objectives. For instance, if you're starting a new project on machine learning applications in healthcare, you could prompt the AI, "Generate 10 innovative ideas for applying machine learning to improve patient care in rural areas." The AI will provide a list of ideas, which you can further explore or refine. Additionally, AI can help you overcome writer's block, offering fresh perspectives and innovative angles you might not have considered on your own.

CODING AND DEBUGGING SUPPORT

In the world of software development, coding and debugging are two of the most time-consuming and critical tasks. Whether you are writing new code or troubleshooting an existing one, AI—particularly through prompt engineering—can play a pivotal role in streamlining and improving these processes. By using well-crafted prompts, you can leverage AI to assist in everything from writing efficient code to identifying and fixing bugs quickly and accurately.

Let's first look at **coding support**. When you're working on a coding project, it's easy to get stuck, whether you're struggling with syntax, trying to implement a new feature, or simply trying to figure out how to structure a particular function. This is where AI comes in. By providing a detailed prompt, you can ask the AI to generate code snippets, help with specific programming languages, or even suggest algorithms. For instance, a prompt like, "Generate Python code to sort a list of dictionaries based on the value of a specific key" is a direct request that AI can fulfill with ease. The AI will not only generate the code but can also offer suggestions for optimizing it or improving performance. You could even ask for specific features, like "Write a function in JavaScript that validates an email address using regular expressions."

AI-driven prompt engineering also extends to more complex coding scenarios. For example, when working with frameworks or libraries, you may want to ask the AI to help you integrate a specific package into your project. A prompt like, "How do I integrate TensorFlow with a Flask application to deploy a machine learning model?" will provide you with step-by-step instructions and example code to help you get the job done.

Next, there's **debugging support**. Debugging can often feel like searching for a needle in a haystack. When errors occur, pinpointing the issue in hundreds or thousands of lines of code can be exhausting and time-consuming. AI, with the help of effective prompts, can assist you by analyzing error messages, suggesting fixes, or even identifying patterns in your code that might cause issues in the future. For example, you could use a prompt such as, "Explain the error message 'IndexError: list index out of range' in Python and suggest ways to fix it." AI will break down the error, explain why it occurred, and offer practical suggestions for resolving it, like checking array bounds or using exception handling.

Furthermore, if you're debugging a piece of code with a specific issue, you can describe the behavior in a prompt to help AI diagnose the problem. A prompt like, "The function I've written doesn't return the expected result. It's supposed to sum the values in a list of dictionaries, but it returns None. Can you help me identify what's wrong?" will trigger a response that walks you through potential causes and solutions, often faster than manual debugging. Additionally, AI can suggest improvements to your error-handling mechanisms, helping you avoid future mistakes.

For **optimization**, AI can also help you improve the efficiency of your code. Once you've written your code, you can ask the AI to analyze it for performance bottlenecks or suggest optimizations. For instance, if your code is running slowly or consuming excessive resources, you might prompt, "How can I optimize this Python function to handle large datasets more efficiently?" The AI can offer suggestions related to memory management, algorithm improvements, or the use of more efficient data structures, ensuring your code runs smoothly and performs at its best.

Code reviews are another area where AI can be invaluable. By feeding your code into an AI system, you can receive immediate feedback on areas that could be improved or optimized. The AI can provide insights into best practices, potential bugs, and even suggest improvements in terms of readability and maintainability.

In addition to assisting with coding and debugging, AI can also play a vital role in **learning new languages** or **frameworks**. For beginners, AI can provide simple explanations and code examples in a new language, helping them understand the syntax and common practices. More advanced developers can ask the AI to generate complex code snippets or provide documentation for specific tools or libraries they're learning to use.

The ability to collaborate with AI for these tasks not only boosts productivity but also allows you to focus more on the creative aspects of software development, knowing that the repetitive or tedious aspects are being handled efficiently. Prompt enginee-ring, when applied to coding and debugging, is an essential tool in modern software development, making it easier for develo-pers at all levels to produce high-quality, error-free software.

CHAPTER 8: CREATIVE USE CASES

AI-powered prompts have unlocked an era of boundless creati-vity, enabling users to bring ideas to life in ways that were once unimaginable. This chapter explores how prompt engineering can serve as a catalyst for storytelling, helping you develop rich narratives and multidimensional characters. It also highlights techniques for crafting art prompts that push generative AI tools to produce stunning visuals aligned with your vision. Additio-nally, we'll dive into brainstorming strategies, demonstrating how AI can act as a creative partner, sparking innovative ideas for any project. By mastering these applications, you'll harness the power of AI to amplify your creative potential.

STORYTELLING AND CHARACTER DEVELOPMENT

In the world of storytelling, the creation of a rich narrative and complex characters is an art that often takes years to perfect. As writers, we aim to captivate readers, to take them on an emotio-nal journey that feels real and meaningful. One of the greatest challenges lies in building characters that resonate with audien-ces—characters that grow, evolve, and reflect the complex na-ture of the human experience. This is where AI and prompt engi-neering step in, offering a new dimension to storytelling by providing powerful tools to explore ideas, refine concepts, and shape narratives more efficiently.

AI, when properly guided through well-structured prompts, can become an invaluable collaborator in the storytelling process. By leveraging the capabilities of large language models (LLMs), such as GPT, writers can prompt AI to generate fresh ideas, develop story arcs, and deepen character complexities in ways that might have taken much longer through traditional methods. It allows you to move beyond writer's block and unlock a flow of creativity that pushes the boundaries of your imagination.

Creating Compelling Characters

Character development is at the heart of any good story. Whether it's a hero who must face a seemingly insurmountable challenge or an antagonist with a hidden agenda, characters are what bring the narrative to life. AI can help writers not only develop a character's personality traits but also their backstories, motivations, fears, and desires. A well-crafted prompt can guide the AI to explore a character's past—what shaped them into who they are, what internal conflicts they might face, and how they interact with other characters in the narrative.

For instance, if you're writing a complex protagonist with conflicting emotions, you can prompt the AI to describe scenarios where these emotions clash, forcing the character to make difficult choices. A simple prompt like "Generate a character struggling with guilt over a past mistake" can lead to a profound exploration of how guilt manifests within the character's actions and relationships. The AI can then generate ideas for dialogue that reflects this internal conflict, suggesting words, phrases, and expressions that sound authentic to the character's voice.

The true power of AI lies in its ability to iterate. By providing a base prompt and adjusting it based on the character's evolving story, the AI can suggest character traits, flaws, and development paths that you might not have originally considered. It's like having a brainstorming partner who can analyze your narrative and suggest deeper layers to the characters, helping you create multidimensional personalities who evolve in ways that feel natural and satisfying.

Building Complex Plot Structures

The plot of a story is the skeleton that holds the narrative together, guiding the characters through their journey. But plot development is a nuanced process. It involves weaving together various elements such as conflict, resolution, pacing, and surprises. AI can assist writers by generating ideas for plot twists, revealing unforeseen consequences of character actions, or even offering alternative story directions.

For example, when you prompt the AI to generate a plot twist, the model can provide options that shift the story in unexpected directions. If you're writing a mystery novel, a well-crafted prompt can lead to the introduction of a red herring or an unexpected revelation that alters the course of the story. You can instruct the AI to think in a specific genre, like "Generate a surprising plot twist for a sci-fi thriller involving time travel," and it will provide suggestions that fit the genre's conventions while still feeling innovative.

AI can also suggest ways to refine the pacing of your plot. By analyzing the flow of the story and identifying areas that may feel too slow or too rushed, the AI can help you adjust scenes to improve the overall rhythm. This can be particularly useful when dealing with complex, nonlinear narratives or stories with multiple points of view, ensuring that each shift in perspective is smooth and engaging.

Dialogue and Interaction

One of the more challenging aspects of writing a story is ensuring that the dialogue feels authentic. Characters speak in unique ways, influenced by their personality, culture, and background. When generating dialogue through AI, the more specific the prompt, the better the outcome. For example, if you're working on a scene where two characters who have a history of conflict come together, you might prompt the AI to generate a conversation where tension is palpable through the dialogue.

Prompt engineering allows you to guide AI to produce dialogue that reflects subtext, tension, and emotional depth. By specifying details like the setting, the character's mood, or their goals in the conversation, you can receive more tailored responses. This is especially beneficial when working on scenes where characters are trying to hide their true emotions or manipulate others through words.

AI can also assist in creating dialogue that enhances the world-building of your story. If your narrative takes place in a futuristic or fantastical setting, you can prompt the AI to generate dialogue that reflects the unique language, slang, or cultural norms of that world. This is an excellent way to make the dialogue feel rooted in the setting, whether it's a post-apocalyptic wasteland or a high-tech utopia.

Interactive Storytelling: Collaboration and Iteration

Perhaps one of the most exciting possibilities with AI and prompt engineering is the potential for interactive storytelling. Writers can engage in a collaborative process where they constantly re-fine and reshape the narrative. By interacting with AI, you create a dynamic relationship where the story evolves in real-time, re-sponding to prompts and shifting based on new ideas or chan-ges in direction. You're no longer alone in crafting the narrative—you have an AI collaborator that helps you test new ideas, flesh out characters, and explore different plot paths.

This level of collaboration is especially useful for writers who struggle with perfectionism or fear of making mistakes. The ite-rative process, aided by AI, allows you to experiment freely wi-thout the fear of writing something "wrong." You can explore dif-ferent character arcs, test various plot structures, and see how different elements fit together, all with the help of your AI part-ner.

The future of storytelling is evolving, and prompt engineering is a powerful tool that can unlock creative potential. By using AI to develop characters, build plotlines, generate dialogue, and re-fine your story, you're tapping into a creative reservoir that acce-lerates your process and expands your imagination. You're not merely outsourcing creativity; you're engaging with an intelligent system that acts as a partner in your artistic journey.

Ultimately, AI's role in storytelling is not to replace the writer but to enhance the creative process. With the right prompts and clear vision, AI can help bring your characters and stories to life in ways that are both unexpected and profoundly impactful.

GENERATING ART PROMPTS FOR AI TOOLS

In the realm of creative expression, AI has revolutionized the pro-cess of art creation, offering an incredibly powerful tool for artists, designers, and creators across various industries. Generating art with AI tools such as DALL·E, MidJourney, and others has become an accessible and exciting way to bring imaginative concepts to life with minimal effort, yet with highly detailed, visually stunning results. However, the magic doesn't lie solely in the power of these AI systems; it's in how you prompt them. The ability to craft precise, effective prompts is the key to unlocking the full potential of AI-generated art.

Let's take a closer look at some of the most prominent AI tools used to generate art:

- **DALL·E (and DALL·E 2)**: Developed by OpenAI, DALL·E is one of the most well-known AI image generators. It's specifically designed to create images from textual descriptions. Its capabilities range from realistic renderings of abstract concepts to whimsical depictions of surreal scenes. You can prompt DALL·E with detailed descriptions, and it will create art that aligns closely with the input, often combining elements that would be difficult to imagine or sketch by hand.

- **MidJourney**: Known for its ability to generate highly artistic, stylized images, MidJourney has become the go-to tool for many artists and designers. It excels at creating dream-like and painterly effects, with an emphasis on vibrant color schemes and imaginative designs. While DALL·E may lean toward a more literal interpretation of prompts, MidJourney embraces an artistic interpretation, often blending reality with a sense of abstraction.

- **Stable Diffusion**: A more recent player in the AI-generated art scene, Stable Diffusion allows users to generate images from text-based prompts, focusing on quality, diversity, and coherence. It's open-source, allowing a large community of creators to experiment and refine its features. Stable Diffusion is often used for a wide range of art styles, from photorealistic imagery to highly stylized, surreal works.

The key to success with any of these platforms is **prompt engineering**—the art of crafting the perfect input that directs the AI to produce exactly what you envision. Different tools have different strengths, so understanding their unique capabilities and how they interpret input will give you an edge.

Crafting Effective Prompts

When generating art with AI, the structure and detail of your prompts can make a world of difference in the outcome. Here are some key aspects to consider when formulating your prompts:

1. Specificity and Detail

The more specific and detailed your prompt is, the more likely you are to get the desired result. For example:

- **Vague Prompt**: "A forest scene."

- **Detailed Prompt**: "A misty forest at dawn with rays of sunlight piercing through tall pine trees, and a small crystal-clear stream running through the center."

Notice how the second prompt provides a rich scene with specifics on the time of day, atmosphere, lighting, and even the details of the environment. This clarity helps the AI better understand the context and generate a more accurate and visually appealing image.

2. Style and Technique

AI tools like MidJourney and DALL·E can create art in various styles, whether it's hyper-realistic, abstract, or impressionistic. If you have a specific style in mind, make sure to incorporate that into your prompt:

- **For Realism**: "A hyper-realistic portrait of a lion with a golden mane, sitting majestically in the savannah under a sunset sky, captured with extreme detail."

- **For Abstract Art**: "An abstract expressionist piece featuring swirling colors and geometric shapes that evoke a sense of movement and energy."

MidJourney excels in generating abstract and surreal imagery, while DALL·E might give you something closer to a realistic version, depending on the wording of your prompt. Understanding the nuances of each AI tool and adjusting your prompts accordingly will yield the best results.

3. Setting the Scene

The setting is crucial in shaping the mood of your image. If you're creating an outdoor scene, specifying elements like the weather, time of day, or even season can impact the feel of the artwork:

- **Prompt with Scene Setting**: "A snowy landscape at twilight with a single glowing cabin in the distance, smoke rising from the chimney, and a starry sky above."

This level of detail gives the AI clear direction on how to combine natural elements with the lighting and mood you wish to evoke.

4. Adding Depth with Emotions and Tone

Art isn't just about objects and places; it's about the feelings it conveys. Adding emotional depth to your prompts can influence the outcome:

- **Mood-Oriented Prompt**: "A hauntingly serene landscape of a lonely mountain peak shrouded in clouds, exuding a sense of isolation and peace."

This simple addition of "hauntingly serene" conveys a mood that will guide the AI to create an image that matches the emotional tone.

5. Experimenting with Concepts and Juxtapositions

AI allows you to blend concepts that might be difficult to imagine or create in traditional art mediums. Experimenting with combinations of contrasting ideas can lead to unexpected and fascinating results:

- **Surreal Prompt**: "A futuristic city skyline blending seamlessly into a lush forest, where trees and skyscrapers coexist, with neon lights casting a soft glow through the trees."

This blending of nature and technology not only creates visual interest but also challenges the AI to merge two worlds in an imaginative way.

Prompt Examples and Tips

Let's explore some sample prompts and how you can tweak them for different AI tools:

- **For DALL·E**: "A cat wearing a space suit, floating in a cosmic environment filled with nebulae and stars, with the Earth visible in the background."

Tip: DALL·E thrives when it receives clear instructions on the scene and elements. Focus on the visual objects and their relationships in the image.

- **For MidJourney**: "A digital painting of a lone wolf in a snowy forest, under a full moon, rendered in the style of a classical oil painting."
Tip: MidJourney excels at interpreting artistic styles. Including terms like "classical oil painting" or "impressionist" helps guide the AI to create more refined, stylized artwork.

- **For Stable Diffusion**: "A steampunk-inspired cityscape with intricate clockwork machinery, glowing copper pipes, and flying airships, during the golden hour."
Tip: Stable Diffusion shines when given detailed context about the setting and technology. Adding mood descriptors like "golden hour" helps set the lighting and atmosphere.

Common Mistakes to Avoid

While crafting your prompts, there are a few common pitfalls to avoid:

1. **Overloading with Information**: While details are important, too many conflicting instructions can confuse the AI. Focus on the core aspects of the image, such as the main subject and the environment.

2. **Ambiguous Language**: Phrases like "make it beautiful" or "create a cool design" are too vague for AI to interpret effectively. Be specific about what you find beautiful or cool (e.g., "a tranquil lake at sunset with golden hues").

3. **Ignoring AI Capabilities**: Each AI has its strengths and weaknesses. MidJourney, for example, is fantastic at surrealism and dream-like art but may not deliver photorealism with the same accuracy as DALL·E.

Generating art with AI is not just about providing a prompt and waiting for results; it's a process of understanding the capabilities of your chosen tool and refining your approach over time. With detailed prompts that specify style, scene, emotion, and even the smallest elements, you can create art that is not only visually stunning but also aligned with your creative vision.

BRAINSTORMING AND IDEATION

Brainstorming and ideation are at the heart of the creative process, and AI tools can significantly enhance both of these stages. When it comes to generating ideas, the traditional method often involves individual thought or group discussions, but AI can expedite this process by offering diverse perspectives quickly and efficiently. Whether you're working on a new project, product design, or marketing campaign, AI-powered brainstorming tools can provide you with a vast array of initial ideas based on input parameters you provide.

In prompt engineering, brainstorming and ideation can be amplified by using AI models like GPT-3 or GPT-4. These models have the ability to analyze trends, identify gaps, and combine concepts in ways that might not occur to a human. For instance, if you're working on a new startup concept, you can ask the AI to generate a list of potential business ideas based on a specific niche, such as eco-friendly products or innovative tech solutions. By specifying parameters like target audience, industry, and technological advancements, you can get tailored sugge-stions that are not only diverse but also feasible.

One of the key advantages of using AI for ideation is its capacity to cross-pollinate ideas from different domains. This is particu-larly helpful for creative professionals who may be stuck in a sin-gle mindset or industry. AI tools can break that cycle by introdu-cing concepts from various fields that are related in unexpected ways. For example, asking an AI to brainstorm content for a mar-keting campaign for a tech company could lead to unique ideas by incorporating trends from the entertainment, fashion, or healthcare sectors.

However, effective brainstorming with AI requires precision in how you phrase your prompts. The more specific you are, the more useful the suggestions will be. A vague prompt like "give me some business ideas" may return general answers that aren't immediately useful, whereas a prompt like "suggest innovative business ideas for a sustainable fashion brand targeting Gen Z in Europe" will give you targeted responses that are immediately actionable. This is where understanding how to structure your prompts becomes crucial in maximizing the creative output of AI.

Another technique to enhance brainstorming with AI is the itera-tive process. You don't have to settle for the first set of ideas the model generates. You can refine your requests, ask for elabora-tion on certain points, or combine multiple suggestions into a more refined concept. This iterative approach is a powerful tool for building a solid foundation for your project, whether it's a new book, an advertisement campaign, or a groundbreaking pro-duct.

One key aspect to remember is that AI tools are best used as a complement to human creativity, not as a replacement. While AI can provide you with an abundance of ideas, the refinement, emotional resonance, and final execution are up to you. Think of AI as your creative assistant, helping you to explore and expand your imagination, while you steer the vision in a direction that aligns with your goals and values.

CHAPTER 9: BUSINESS AND PRODUCTIVITY

AI is revolutionizing the way businesses operate, offering tools that can save time, increase efficiency, and open up new possibilities. In this chapter, you'll explore how prompt engineering can automate workflows, from scheduling tasks to managing data flows seamlessly. You'll also discover how prompts enhance customer service, enabling AI to deliver personalized, accurate, and timely responses that elevate user experiences. Additionally, we'll delve into the role of AI in education and e-learning, showing how well-crafted prompts can make learning more engaging, accessible, and tailored to individual needs. Whether you're streamlining workflows, enhancing client interactions, or transforming educational experiences, AI-driven solutions offer a wealth of opportunities to drive meaningful change.

AUTOMATING WORKFLOWS WITH PROMPTS

Automating workflows with prompts is one of the most powerful applications of AI in today's fast-paced business environment. When we talk about workflow automation, we're referring to using technology to handle repetitive or time-consuming tasks, allowing employees to focus on more strategic and creative work. With AI, particularly prompt engineering, we can streamline a wide range of processes across industries—from customer service to content creation, from data analysis to marketing campaigns.

At its core, workflow automation with AI relies on creating well-defined prompts that instruct AI models to perform specific tasks. These prompts trigger the AI to execute actions, analyze data, respond to queries, or even generate content. The key to making this work seamlessly is crafting prompts that are clear, context-aware, and optimized for the particular task at hand. Poorly constructed prompts can lead to inefficiencies, errors, or irrelevant results, whereas well-designed prompts allow for smooth and efficient automation.

Examples of Workflow Automation Using Prompts

1. **Customer Service Chatbots**: Imagine an AI chatbot designed to handle initial customer inquiries. Instead of waiting for a human to respond to each customer request, you can set up a prompt system that allows the AI to analyze a customer's query and provide an instant response. For example, a simple prompt like "What is your issue with the product?" can be programmed to recognize keywords like "refund," "shipping," or "damaged," and the AI can automatically suggest the appropriate solution. With more complex queries, the AI can gather preliminary information and hand it off to a human agent for further resolution.

2. **Email Filtering and Response**: AI-powered email systems can automate sorting, categorizing, and

responding to incoming emails based on predefined prompts. For instance, a prompt could be set up to analyze the subject line or content of the email and trigger actions based on keywords. An email asking for a product demo could generate an automated response with a scheduling link, while a customer complaint could trigger an automatic acknowledgment response, ensuring that no email is left unattended. This kind of automation can save countless hours, especially in environments with high volumes of emails.

3. **Data Analysis**: In data-driven workflows, AI can be used to automate the process of sorting through large datasets and providing actionable insights. Consider a scenario where a company needs to analyze customer feedback collected from surveys. By creating a set of prompts that instruct the AI to identify common themes or sentiment within the responses, you can automate the summarization and categorization process. A prompt like "Analyze the sentiment of the following feedback" can trigger the AI to run sentiment analysis algorithms, sorting feedback into positive, neutral, and negative categories automatically. The result is a much faster turnaround time on actionable insights that can drive business decisions.

4. **Content Scheduling and Social Media Management**: In the context of digital marketing, AI can automate the scheduling of content, ensuring posts are timely and consistent across various platforms. Prompts can be set up to check social media calendars, post at optimal times, and even generate short snippets or headlines for posts based on the content of the day. For example, you

can set a prompt like "Generate a tweet about the upco-ming webinar on AI prompt engineering," and the AI will create a relevant and engaging post, automatically sche-duled to go live at the best time for audience engage-ment.

Best Practices for Workflow Automation with Prompts

To truly take advantage of AI in workflow automation, you need to adhere to a few best practices for prompt design:

- **Be Specific**: The more specific your prompt is, the better the AI will perform. Instead of a general prompt like "Au-tomate customer service responses," a more specific prompt such as "Respond to shipping inquiries with the tracking link and delivery estimate" will yield more accu-rate results.

- **Test and Refine**: Workflow automation is an iterative pro-cess. After creating your prompts, test them in real-world scenarios to ensure they produce the desired outcomes. If the AI isn't providing the expected results, refine the prompts. Sometimes slight adjustments in wording or structure can lead to significantly better performance.

- **Incorporate Human Oversight**: While automation can handle a wide range of tasks, it's still important to moni-tor the AI's performance, especially in cases that require complex judgment. Automated workflows should be de-signed in such a way that human intervention is available when needed.

- **Integrate with Existing Systems**: The most efficient workflows integrate AI prompts with your company's exi-sting software tools, like CRM systems, email platforms, or project management tools. This seamless integration ensures that AI-driven workflows are part of the broader organizational infrastructure.

The Future of Workflow Automation

The future of workflow automation is poised to become even more advanced, as AI models become increasingly sophisticated in their ability to handle a wider array of tasks. As businesses continue to adopt AI-driven tools, the need for well-crafted prompts will only increase. Developing a deep understanding of how to create effective prompts will give you a significant advantage in automating workflows, improving efficiency, and unlocking new possibilities for innovation within your organization.

In conclusion, automating workflows with prompts isn't just about saving time; it's about empowering businesses to operate more efficiently, improve accuracy, and free up human resources for higher-level tasks. By understanding how to design and implement effective prompts, you'll be well-positioned to take advantage of the full potential of AI in your business processes.

CUSTOMER SERVICE APPLICATIONS

Customer service applications powered by AI and prompt engineering are transforming the way businesses interact with their customers. These applications not only enhance customer satisfaction but also streamline operations, providing quicker, more accurate responses while reducing the burden on human agents. In this section, we'll dive into the different ways AI and prompt engineering are being applied in customer service, how prompts can be optimized to improve outcomes, and real-world examples that showcase the power of these tools.

How AI Enhances Customer Service

At its core, AI in customer service involves automating tasks that typically require human interaction, such as answering frequently asked questions, resolving simple issues, and guiding customers through processes. AI can be used across various channels, including live chat, email, voice assistants, and even social media platforms. However, the key to successfully implementing AI in these channels is crafting effective prompts that guide the AI in delivering the most relevant and helpful responses.

For instance, imagine an AI-powered chatbot integrated into an e-commerce website. The AI could be programmed to help customers track orders, find product recommendations, or handle basic queries. But to ensure the chatbot delivers accurate and helpful answers, you need precise prompts that define the scope of each possible interaction.

Designing Effective Prompts for Customer Service

The effectiveness of AI-driven customer service largely depends on the quality of the prompts used. Prompts should be designed to allow the AI to understand the customer's intent clearly and provide the most appropriate response. This requires not just simple language but context-aware prompts that factor in nuances such as customer sentiment, urgency, and the specifics of the inquiry.

For example, a generic prompt like "What is your issue?" could result in a vague or insufficient answer. Instead, a more refined prompt could be "Can you tell me if you need help with an order, a product, or account information?" This directs the AI to focus its response and allows the system to retrieve relevant information more quickly.

The AI can also be trained to recognize more complex customer queries by providing detailed instructions in the prompt. For instance, if a customer asks, "How do I return a defective item?", the prompt could guide the AI to recognize keywords like "return" and "defective" and respond with clear, actionable steps based on the company's return policy.

Real-World Examples of AI in Customer Service

Let's explore some practical examples to better understand how AI and prompt engineering improve customer service applications:

Automated Help Desks: Many companies have implemented AI-driven help desks to assist customers in resolving technical issues. For example, a telecom company might use an AI system to diagnose and resolve common connectivity issues. By setting up prompts such as "Is your internet connection down?", "Have you restarted your router?", and "Please check your cables," the AI can quickly guide the customer through troubleshooting steps. The AI can even detect common problems by asking specific questions based on previous interactions, ensuring that the user doesn't have to repeat themselves.

Personalized Recommendations: AI systems can also be used to suggest products, services, or solutions based on customer behavior or past interactions. For instance, in an online retail scenario, an AI system can ask, "What kind of product are you looking for today? Are you interested in electronics, clothing, or home goods?" Based on the user's response, the system can further narrow down the search with additional prompts like, "Do you need a specific brand?" or

"Would you like to see customer reviews before making your decision?"

Voice Assistants and Interactive IVR Systems: In customer service call centers, AI-driven voice assistants are becoming increasingly common. With an Interactive Voice Response (IVR) system, customers can interact with the AI system via spoken language to resolve common issues. An example prompt could be, "Please state the reason for your call: billing, technical support, or account inquiries." Once the AI identifies the customer's need, it can route them to the appropriate department or even provide automated solutions without the need for a live agent. AI can also offer suggestions, like "I see you're calling about your bill. Would you like to know your balance or set up a payment plan?"

Sentiment Analysis for Customer Satisfaction: AI can also play a crucial role in identifying customer sentiment through text or speech analysis. For example, a chatbot could prompt a customer after providing an answer or solution with a simple question: "Was this answer helpful to you?" Based on the response, the AI can identify negative sentiment or dissatisfaction by analyzing the language used. If a customer responds with a phrase like "I'm still confused" or "That didn't help at all," the AI can escalate the issue to a human representative to ensure the problem is resolved. Such sentiment-aware prompts allow companies to respond proactively to issues and prevent escalation.

The Role of AI-Powered Self-Service

Another growing trend in customer service is AI-powered self-service. By providing customers with the tools they need to resolve issues on their own, companies can reduce operational costs and improve customer satisfaction. AI chatbots and virtual assistants are often used to guide users through self-service processes such as resetting passwords, finding tracking information, or canceling subscriptions.

For example, a customer might ask an AI assistant, "How do I reset my password?" The AI could then prompt with, "Please provide your registered email address," followed by a series of steps to reset the password automatically. This kind of automation allows customers to solve their issues independently without waiting for a human agent to assist, leading to quicker resolutions.

Best Practices for AI in Customer Service

To get the best out of AI in customer service, there are some best practices to follow:

- **Clarity and Precision**: The prompts used in customer service applications should be clear, precise, and easy for customers to understand. Ambiguity in prompts leads to confusion, which can hinder the customer experience.

- **Context Awareness**: AI systems should be aware of the context of the conversation. For example, if a customer previously asked about a product return, the AI should follow up on that topic rather than starting a new conversation from scratch.

- **Continuous Improvement**: It's important to continuously monitor and improve AI-driven customer service. Regularly evaluate how well your AI is performing by reviewing customer feedback and tweaking the prompts as needed.

- **Human Oversight**: While AI can handle many customer service tasks, human oversight is essential for more complex or emotional issues. Ensure that your AI system can seamlessly transfer customers to human agents when necessary.

Future Trends in AI Customer Service

As AI continues to evolve, we can expect even greater advancements in customer service applications. One area of growth is the integration of AI with advanced machine learning models to predict customer needs before they even arise. This predictive capability will allow companies to offer highly personalized experiences, ensuring that customers receive timely solutions to their problems. With natural language processing (NLP) and emotional intelligence capabilities, future AI systems will not only answer questions but also respond empathetically, creating more human-like interactions.

AI-powered customer service applications, guided by well-engineered prompts, have the potential to significantly improve the efficiency, accuracy, and overall experience for customers. By automating routine tasks and providing quick, relevant solutions, AI can empower businesses to meet customer expectations more effectively while freeing up human agents to focus on more complex and value-added tasks. As this technology continues to evolve, the opportunities for optimizing customer service workflows will only expand, creating new ways for businesses to connect with and support their customers.

AI IN EDUCATION AND E-LEARNING

AI in education and e-learning is revolutionizing the way we approach teaching and learning. The traditional methods of education, while valuable, often come with limitations such as one-size-fits-all teaching approaches, limited feedback, and restricted access to resources. AI, on the other hand, offers personalized, scalable solutions that can address the diverse needs of students and enhance the overall educational experience. In this section, we will explore how AI is being utilized in education, the role of prompt engineering in optimizing learning tools, and practical examples that demonstrate how AI is making a difference in both classroom settings and online learning environments.

Personalizing Learning with AI

One of the most powerful applications of AI in education is personalization. Each student has their own learning style, pace, and preferences, which traditional classroom settings often fail to accommodate. With AI, it is possible to create highly tailored educational experiences that adapt in real-time to the needs of individual learners.

For instance, AI-powered educational tools can analyze a student's progress, identify areas where they may be struggling, and adjust the difficulty level of tasks or offer additional resources to reinforce learning. In this context, prompt engineering plays a crucial role. By crafting specific, context-aware prompts, educators and AI developers can guide the AI in providing relevant feedback and recommendations based on the student's responses. For example, imagine an AI tutoring system for mathematics. A prompt could be constructed as follows: *"Based on your answer to the previous question, it seems like you are having trouble with algebraic expressions. Would you like to try a few practice problems focusing on simplifying equations?"* This prompt is personalized because it directly responds to the student's progress, offering a targeted solution that meets the student's specific learning needs.

AI-Powered Feedback and Assessment

Feedback is an essential component of the learning process. Traditionally, feedback has been a time-consuming task for educators, and in large classrooms, it's often delayed or insufficient. AI, however, can provide immediate, constructive feedback, enabling students to improve continuously. With well-engineered prompts, AI systems can evaluate student responses and give feedback on everything from grammar to problem-solving strategies.

Consider an AI-driven language learning platform. A student might submit a written assignment in Spanish, and the AI can analyze the text for errors in grammar, vocabulary, and sentence structure. The AI can then generate a prompt, such as: *"I noticed that you used 'yo tener' instead of 'yo tengo.' Would you like to review the correct conjugation of the verb 'tener'?"* This prompt serves both as a correction and as an invitation to engage with the learning material. It's a specific, actionable response that helps the student correct their mistake and understand why it was incorrect.

Beyond grammar and language, AI can also assess students' problem-solving approaches in fields like mathematics, science, and even the arts. For example, an AI system in a coding class could analyze a student's code and provide feedback: *"Your algorithm works, but it could be more efficient. Would you like a hint on optimizing the loop structure?"* This kind of real-time feedback can be more impactful than traditional methods, where students might have to wait for days or weeks to receive feedback from a teacher.

Adaptive Learning Environments

Another significant advantage of AI in education is the creation of adaptive learning environments. These environments adjust based on the learner's needs, providing the right amount of challenge at the right time. Instead of following a rigid curriculum, AI-based platforms can continuously evolve the content and pacing according to the student's mastery level.

For instance, an AI tutor in an e-learning platform might start by assessing a student's baseline knowledge through a short quiz or diagnostic test. Based on the results, the system will tailor the lessons to address areas where the student needs improvement, while providing more advanced materials in areas where the student excels. Through the use of dynamic prompts, the system can ask questions such as: *"You've mastered basic fractions. Would you like to move on to decimal operations?"* or *"It seems you're struggling with solving equations. Would you like to review how to balance both sides?"* By responding to the student's learning path, the AI ensures that the learner is neither overwhelmed nor underchallenged, creating an optimal educational experience.

Supporting Teachers and Educators

AI in education doesn't just benefit students; it also supports teachers by automating administrative tasks and providing insights into student performance. Educators can use AI to track student progress, identify patterns, and get recommendations on how to best address individual learning needs. For example, AI tools can analyze test results and flag students who are at risk of falling behind. Based on this data, AI could generate prompts to guide the teacher: *"Student X has scored consistently low in the algebra section. Would you like to suggest a targeted review session on linear equations?"* This allows the teacher to act proactively, ensuring no student is left behind.

Furthermore, AI-powered tools can assist with grading, especially in subjects that require objective assessments such as multiple-choice questions or quizzes. These tools can also analyze open-ended responses to identify common mistakes or gaps in understanding. In this case, prompt engineering would focus on ensuring the AI can distinguish between correct and incorrect answers accurately, as well as provide feedback that is both relevant and educational.

AI-Driven Content Creation and Curriculum Design

AI is also becoming a key player in content creation for education. By analyzing student performance and preferences, AI can help educators design personalized curriculum materials that cater to the needs of their students. For example, AI could generate quizzes, assignments, and even interactive lessons based on the topics that students are currently studying. By analyzing patterns in student behavior and engagement, AI can suggest which topics might require more focus and which are better understood. For example, a teacher may use an AI system to create a custom worksheet for students studying biology. The AI could prompt: *"Based on recent lesson plans, I suggest a worksheet focusing on cellular respiration for students who have been struggling with that topic."* The prompt is generated based on both the curriculum and real-time student data, ensuring that the educational content is timely, relevant, and appropriately challenging.

Gamification in Education

AI also plays a crucial role in gamifying the learning experience, which can significantly boost student engagement and motivation. AI can create personalized challenges and rewards, making learning more interactive and fun. By using game-like elements

such as points, levels, badges, and competitions, AI systems can turn learning into a dynamic, engaging experience.

For example, an AI system could design a series of challenges based on the material a student is studying, such as math puzzles or vocabulary quizzes. As the student progresses, the system might prompt: *"You've reached level 3 in the math challenge! Are you ready to tackle the next set of problems, or would you like to review level 2 before proceeding?"* This keeps the student engaged while promoting active learning.

Future Trends and Challenges

As AI continues to evolve, the potential applications in education are vast. From creating fully interactive, immersive learning environments to integrating AI with virtual and augmented reality, the possibilities are limitless. However, there are also challenges to consider, such as ensuring that AI tools are accessible to all students, regardless of socioeconomic background, and that they are designed to be fair and unbiased.

One key area of future development is the integration of AI with emotional intelligence. By recognizing and responding to students' emotions—such as frustration, boredom, or excitement—AI could provide a more empathetic and supportive learning experience. Imagine an AI tutor that detects when a student is struggling and offers encouragement, or one that adjusts the difficulty of tasks based on how stressed or engaged a student seems.

The integration of AI into education is still in its early stages, but its potential to revolutionize the way we teach and learn is undeniable. By harnessing the power of AI and prompt engineering, we can unlock new possibilities for education in the digital age.

CHALLENGES AND FUTURE TRENDS

CHAPTER 10: ETHICAL CONSIDERATIONS

As AI becomes an integral part of daily life, ethical considerations take center stage. Ensuring fairness, transparency, and accountability in AI systems is not just a technical challenge but a societal responsibility. This chapter examines the complexities of bias in AI responses, exploring how unintended prejudices arise from data and prompt design. We'll discuss strategies for writing responsible prompts that encourage balanced and ethical outputs. Finally, we'll emphasize the importance of human oversight, highlighting your role in guiding AI toward decisions that align with ethical principles and real-world needs, ensuring AI serves everyone equitably.

BIAS IN AI RESPONSES

Bias in AI responses is one of the most critical issues we face today as AI continues to shape various sectors. But what does "bias" really mean in the context of artificial intelligence?

At its core, bias in AI refers to the ways in which AI systems, particularly language models, can produce outputs that are systematically unfair or skewed based on certain factors. These biases arise from the data the AI is trained on, which often reflects the biases present in society, culture, and historical context. If an AI is trained on data that contains stereotypes or imbalances, it can end up reinforcing these patterns in its responses, even unintentionally.

For example, imagine you're using an AI to generate job candidate recommendations. If the training data includes past hiring practices that favored one gender or ethnic group over others, the AI may inadvertently recommend candidates that align with those biases, even though the ideal candidate should be selected based on qualifications and skill alone. This is a classic case of gender bias or racial bias creeping into AI systems, resulting in recommendations that are not fair or equitable.

Another example might involve language use in AI. If an AI has been trained primarily on texts that employ outdated or stereotypical language, it could replicate that language in its responses. For instance, when generating text about leadership, it might only reference male pronouns or cite historical male leaders, inadvertently reinforcing the stereotype that leadership is primarily a male domain.

Bias can also manifest in more subtle ways, such as reinforcing societal norms or failing to accommodate diverse perspectives.

For instance, an AI might produce content that aligns more with Western values while ignoring or misunderstanding non-Western cultures, thus making its responses less applicable or relevant in global contexts.

The good news is that these biases are not insurmountable. By understanding where they come from and how they show up in AI outputs, we can take steps to mitigate them. One key way to do this is by diversifying the data that is used to train AI models. The more diverse the dataset, the more likely it is that the AI will produce responses that are fair and representative of a wide range of viewpoints. Additionally, the implementation of fairness-aware algorithms and regular audits of AI models can help ensure that biases do not slip through unnoticed.

It's also important to consider the type of prompts used. Bias can also creep into the responses of AI models if prompts are not carefully constructed. For instance, a poorly worded prompt can unintentionally guide the model towards biased outputs. Being mindful of how questions and requests are framed can reduce the chance of generating biased or unfair responses.

Ultimately, the responsibility for mitigating bias in AI lies not just with the developers and researchers who build the systems, but also with all of us who interact with them. By being aware of potential biases and asking the right questions, we can actively help in shaping a future where AI serves everyone fairly and equitably.

Bias in AI is not just a technical issue—it's a societal one. As AI continues to play an ever-growing role in our lives, ensuring that it operates without perpetuating harmful biases is crucial for building trust in these systems and ensuring that they contribute positively to society as a whole.

WRITING RESPONSIBLE PROMPTS

Writing responsible prompts is an essential skill when working with AI, particularly when it comes to maintaining ethical standards and ensuring that the generated outputs align with our values. A responsible prompt isn't just about asking the right question; it's about framing that question in a way that minimizes harm, avoids biases, and encourages positive, inclusive results. When you craft prompts, you're not just guiding the AI, you're shaping the outcome, and with great power comes great responsibility.

First, let's define what makes a prompt "responsible." A responsible prompt is one that is clear, specific, and mindful of the potential implications of the AI's response. It avoids leading questions or any language that might cause the AI to generate harmful, biased, or offensive content. But, more importantly, it encourages productive, fair, and thoughtful answers.

For example, consider a prompt like: "What are the most successful leadership traits for women in business?" While this seems like a reasonable question, it implicitly introduces a bias—suggesting that leadership traits might differ between genders. A more responsible version might be: "What are the most successful leadership traits in business?" This framing allows the AI to explore the concept of leadership without making assumptions based on gender, thus generating more universally applicable advice.

One of the biggest challenges in writing responsible prompts is being aware of implicit biases—both those that you may introduce into the prompt itself and those that may arise from the AI's training data. Bias can creep in when we make assumptions in our wording. For instance, phrases like "best chef" or "most skilled programmer" can unintentionally reinforce gender or racial stereotypes, even if they aren't explicitly stated. To avoid this, it's crucial to write prompts that are neutral and inclusive. Instead of asking, "What are the qualities of the best male engineers?" ask, "What qualities are important for great engineers?" This removes any unnecessary gender bias and ensures that the prompt is inclusive of all possible perspectives.

Another key aspect of writing responsible prompts is clarity. AI models rely heavily on the specificity of the prompt to produce accurate and relevant outputs. If the question is vague, the results will be equally vague. A clear and responsible prompt eliminates ambiguity, making it easier for the AI to understand your intentions and provide useful, focused responses.

Take the prompt: "Tell me about the history of technology." This is quite broad and could lead to a general or unfocused response. A more specific prompt would be: "What are the key technological advancements of the 20th century and their impact on society?" The second version gives the AI more direction and ensures the response is more detailed and relevant to your needs.

Another critical factor in writing responsible prompts is being mindful of context. AI doesn't have a full understanding of the world like humans do—it doesn't have common sense or cultural nuances unless explicitly trained to recognize them. This means that when you write prompts, you must be very precise in specifying the context, especially when asking for advice, opinions, or subjective analysis. For instance, asking, "What is the best way to treat mental health?" could lead to a response that isn't tailored to specific cultural or individual needs. A more responsible prompt might be: "What are some well-researched, effective approaches to managing anxiety in adults, specifically in urban environments?" This prompt is more specific, takes into account the type of disorder, and even the context of the environment.

When writing responsible prompts, it's also important to consider the impact of the response. Will the AI's output help or harm the situation? Will it encourage positive change or reinforce harmful stereotypes? This requires us to anticipate the potential effects of the AI's responses and ensure that we are guiding the model toward generating outputs that are constructive. For example, if you're asking for relationship advice, instead of asking, "What should I do if my partner is always angry?" which could result in overly simplistic or potentially harmful responses, you could ask, "What are some healthy ways to approach conflict resolution in relationships?" This ensures that the AI's answer promotes positive, healthy behaviors.

Ultimately, responsible prompting is about being intentional. You need to think about the broader implications of your questions. Will the answer promote inclusivity and understanding, or will it perpetuate harmful ideas? Can the prompt be interpreted in multiple ways, and if so, how can it be framed more clearly to guide the AI's response in a desired direction?

To sum it up, writing responsible prompts isn't just about avoiding mistakes—it's about proactively designing questions that encourage fairness, clarity, and positivity. By keeping biases in check, being specific and clear, and being conscious of the broader impacts of the AI's responses, you help steer AI-generated content toward the kinds of outcomes that benefit everyone. It's a powerful tool, but it's up to us to wield it responsibly.

THE ROLE OF HUMAN OVERSIGHT

The role of human oversight in AI systems cannot be overstated. As powerful and advanced as AI technologies have become, they are still far from perfect. They rely on complex algorithms and vast datasets, which can sometimes lead to unintended or suboptimal outcomes. Human oversight ensures that AI-generated results are not only accurate but also aligned with ethical standards, societal norms, and the values of the users it serves.

Human involvement is essential for interpreting AI outputs within the context of real-world complexities. AI models, such as large language models, operate based on patterns observed in data, but they lack true understanding or judgment. This can lead to responses that might be technically correct in a narrow sense but are not suitable for a broader, real-world application. Here, human oversight steps in to provide the necessary context and nuance.

For instance, consider an AI-driven tool used in hiring processes. The AI might review resumes and rank candidates based on various factors. However, without human oversight, the AI could inadvertently reinforce biases present in the data. It might favor certain demographic characteristics over others, based on patterns found in historical hiring practices. Human oversight is critical in this context to ensure that fairness, diversity, and inclusion are prioritized, and any biased recommendations are identified and corrected before they impact decisions.

The need for human oversight is especially crucial in the creative industries. AI-generated content, such as in writing, art, and music, can offer impressive results, but the interpretation and value of that content depend on the human touch. When AI generates a story or a character, it lacks the emotional depth, cultural sensitivity, and creative intuition that a human writer or artist can provide. Human oversight ensures that AI-generated creations are not only technically competent but also emotionally resonant and socially responsible. It's the human creator who will ask the crucial questions: Does this story honor the intended message? Are the characters relatable, or do they reinforce harmful stereotypes? Is the content accessible to diverse audiences?

Even in more technical domains, such as medical diagnostics, AI tools can help identify patterns in patient data or suggest potential diagnoses. However, these suggestions must be reviewed by qualified professionals to ensure their relevance and accuracy in a specific patient context. A physician's oversight helps interpret the AI's suggestions, making sure they align with the patient's unique circumstances, medical history, and needs. An AI tool might flag a condition, but it is up to the human expert to validate, dismiss, or refine that finding.

Another important aspect of human oversight is the ability to handle edge cases—situations that the AI may not have encountered in its training data or that fall outside the parameters the AI was designed to handle. For example, if an AI system is generating recommendations based on user preferences, it might struggle to provide accurate suggestions for a user whose tastes are vastly different from those of the majority in the dataset. In these situations, human intervention is crucial to guide the AI's decision-making process and ensure that it continues to function appropriately, even in unfamiliar scenarios.

Human oversight also plays a role in ensuring that AI systems comply with laws, regulations, and ethical standards. As AI technologies evolve, so too do the frameworks governing their use. For example, laws regarding data privacy, intellectual property, and discrimination continue to change. Without human oversight, AI systems might inadvertently violate these laws, whether by using personal data inappropriately or by creating biased outcomes. A human overseeing the system can flag potential issues, mitigate risks, and ensure compliance with relevant legislation.

Moreover, human oversight helps prevent misuse or abuse of AI technologies. While AI can be a powerful tool, it can also be weaponized or used for malicious purposes. For example, AI-generated deepfakes can be used to spread misinformation or defamation. Having human experts in place to identify and prevent harmful uses of AI is vital to ensuring the responsible deployment of these technologies.

It's also important to note that human oversight is not a passive role—it requires active engagement and critical thinking. Simply checking the output of an AI system is not enough. Human experts need to continuously monitor AI processes, assess whether the outputs are appropriate for the intended context, and be ready to intervene if something goes wrong. This ongoing feedback loop allows AI systems to improve over time, as human input helps correct errors and refine performance.

However, human oversight is not without its challenges. One of the main difficulties is the potential for humans to inadvertently introduce their own biases into the review process. If human experts are not aware of their own prejudices, they might unintentionally allow these biases to influence their judgment of AI-generated outputs. To combat this, training programs for those overseeing AI systems should emphasize the importance of self-awareness, objectivity, and ethical decision-making. Additionally, the development of diverse oversight teams, with different perspectives and experiences, can help counteract individual biases and ensure that AI outputs are more fair and inclusive.

Whether in creative endeavors, business decisions, healthcare, or any other field, human oversight gua-rantees that AI outputs are relevant, accurate, ethical, and ali-gned with the needs and values of society. By working hand-in-hand with AI, we can unlock its full potential while safeguar-ding against its limitations.

CHAPTER 11: MANAGING AI LIMITATIONS AND MODEL ISSUES

While AI systems have revolutionized how we interact with technology, they are not without their limitations and quirks. Every AI model, no matter how advanced, operates within certain boundaries defined by its training data, architecture, and inherent design. In this chapter, we'll delve into the practical challenges that arise when working with AI, such as understanding its limitations, handling inconsistencies in responses, and resolving unexpected outputs.

By exploring these topics, you'll gain insights and strategies to navigate these obstacles effectively, ensuring smoother interactions and more reliable outcomes in your work with AI systems.

UNDERSTANDING AI LIMITATIONS

Understanding the limitations of AI is crucial for anyone working with these systems. While the progress in artificial intelligence has been impressive, it's essential to remember that these systems are still bound by specific constraints. These limitations often stem from various factors like the quality of data, the structure of the model, and how well it can generalize to new scenarios. Let's break down some of the key limitations you should be aware of when working with AI.

Data Dependency

One of the primary limitations of AI is its reliance on data. AI models, particularly large language models (LLMs), are trained on vast datasets, and their performance is tightly connected to the quality and scope of the data they've seen. This means that AI can only generate responses based on patterns it has learned from past data. If the data is biased, incomplete, or lacks sufficient diversity, the AI's outputs will reflect these flaws. For example, an AI trained primarily on English-language sources might struggle to understand or generate accurate responses in other languages or dialects, or it may provide responses that are culturally or contextually off-mark.

Example:

Imagine you're using an AI to translate a phrase from English to French. If the training data didn't include a wide variety of French expressions or regional language differences, the translation could be overly formal or miss important contextual nuances, leading to a less accurate or inappropriate result.

Understanding Context

AI models are exceptional at processing language and understanding patterns within that language. However, they often struggle with deep context. While AI can follow syntax and make connections based on the immediate prompt, it may fail to grasp the broader context, especially if that context isn't explicitly provided in the prompt itself. This can lead to misunderstandings or outputs that miss the mark.

Example:

You might prompt the AI with the question, "What did John do after he arrived?" The AI may generate a valid response based on text seen during training, but it might not have the deeper understanding of the situation, such as whether "John" refers to a specific person in your life or to a character in a book. Without clear context, the AI's answer may be far from accurate.

Lack of Common Sense and Reasoning

Despite their impressive capabilities, AI models do not possess the ability to reason in the same way humans do. They can process language, generate predictions, and apply learned patterns, but they do not have an inherent understanding of the world. They rely on data, not lived experience or intuition. This leads to situations where the AI might generate responses that are logically coherent based on the input but may not be practically useful or appropriate in real-life scenarios.

Example:

Imagine you ask an AI, "Can I leave a cake in the oven overnight?" The AI may generate a logically plausible response based on past patterns, but it may miss the fact that such an action would likely ruin the cake and possibly create safety hazards. It doesn't understand the real-world implications like a human would, even if it has encountered similar phrases in its training data.

Inability to Handle Ambiguity Well

AI systems are good at processing clear, straightforward inputs but often struggle with ambiguity. If a prompt lacks clear direction or has multiple meanings, the AI might default to a guess based on its training, which may not always align with your intended meaning. This is why being specific and clear in your prompts is so essential.

Example:

If you ask an AI, "What's the best way to improve performance?", the model might generate general advice based on a wide variety of contexts. However, without specifying the type of performance (e.g., work, athletic, mental), the output might be less useful or completely off-base.

Inability to Learn in Real-Time

Most AI systems, particularly language models, do not have the capability to learn or adapt in real-time based on new information outside of the training period. Once a model has been trained, it doesn't learn from individual interactions unless specifically retrained. This means that AI is static until a model update occurs.

Example:

If you were to train an AI system to recognize a new word or concept that has just emerged, the AI wouldn't instantly understand or incorporate it. For instance, a new technological term or internet meme might not be part of the model's knowledge until the model is retrained on fresh data containing that information.

Overfitting and Generalization

AI models often face a challenge known as overfitting, where they memorize specific patterns from the training data rather than generalizing to new, unseen data. While overfitting can result in high performance on the training data, it can lead to poor generalization when confronted with novel inputs. This is particularly an issue in highly specialized tasks where the model might focus too much on details that don't apply to a wider context.

Example:

If you use a model trained exclusively on medical texts to diagnose conditions, the model might give impressively accurate answers for conditions it's seen in the data. However, if presented with a rare condition or a novel symptom combination that wasn't represented in the training data, the AI could struggle to provide a reliable diagnosis.

Ethical and Bias Constraints

AI systems can inherit biases from the data they are trained on. These biases can range from gender or racial biases to more subtle cultural or ideological biases. A model trained on data that reflects historical inequalities may inadvertently perpetuate or amplify these issues in its responses. Understanding this limitation is crucial to ensure fairness, especially when AI is used for decision-making processes that can have real-world consequences, such as hiring or lending.

Example:

A hiring AI that was trained on resumes from a particular demographic might prioritize candidates from that demographic, even if the training data didn't explicitly reflect that bias. This can lead to biased outputs that reinforce societal disparities, even though the AI itself has no intent to discriminate.

Computational Constraints

Another limitation is the computational resources required for running advanced AI models. While models like GPT-3 are powerful, they are also extremely resource-intensive, requiring considerable computational power to function efficiently. In certain environments with limited resources (such as mobile devices), the AI's ability to perform well may be restricted, limiting its accessibility and utility.

Example:

An AI-based app designed to run on a smartphone might not be able to generate high-quality responses or interact seamlessly due to hardware limitations. This becomes especially relevant when trying to use AI in real-time applications that demand both speed and accuracy.

While AI technology has brought about remarkable advancements, understanding its limitations is essential for effectively using it in real-world applications. Acknowledging these constraints—such as data reliance, lack of reasoning, and ambiguity handling—ensures you are better prepared to work with AI models in a way that is practical and realistic. By recognizing these limitations, you can refine your approaches, write better prompts, and ultimately manage your expectations of AI, leading to more efficient and accurate outcomes. Always remember, AI is a powerful tool, but it requires careful handling and continuous oversight to unlock its full potential.

OVERCOMING MODEL INCONSISTENCIES

One of the most common challenges when working with AI models is their inherent inconsistencies. These inconsistencies arise for various reasons and can make the output less reliable, especially when you are relying on AI for tasks that require precision and consistency. In this section, we will explore the causes of these inconsistencies and practical strategies for overcoming them.

Variability in Responses

One of the primary issues with AI models, particularly those based on natural language processing (NLP), is their tendency to generate varied responses to similar prompts. This variability can be frustrating when you are seeking a consistent and predictable outcome. For instance, if you ask the model the same question multiple times, you may get different answers each time, even though the prompt is identical.

This issue stems from the probabilistic nature of models like GPT, which do not simply choose the most likely response but instead generate a range of possible answers based on their training data. The model's responses are influenced by various factors, including the temperature setting, the randomness introduced during training, and the context it has been given.

Example:

Imagine you ask an AI model, "What is the capital of France?" At one time, the model might respond with "Paris," but another time, it might say "Paris is the capital of France," or it could even generate a more detailed answer with additional facts. These variations may not always be harmful, but in certain applications—such as customer service or legal advice—precision is crucial.

Inconsistent Understanding of Context

AI models rely heavily on context to generate relevant and coherent responses. However, they often struggle with maintaining context over longer conversations or more complex scenarios. Inconsistent context understanding can lead to answers that seem irrelevant or disconnected from the original query.

For example, if you're interacting with an AI model over several turns and the context shifts subtly, the AI might not always pick up on those shifts. As a result, its response might seem out of place, leading to confusion or inaccuracies.

Example:

Let's say you ask an AI, "What is the weather like today?" followed by, "How should I dress for the weather?" The model should ideally recognize that you are still referring to the weather from the previous question. However, if the model loses track of this context, it might give a generic response, such as "Wear something comfortable," instead of tailoring its answer to the specific weather conditions.

Ambiguity in Prompt Design

Ambiguous prompts are another significant source of inconsistency. If your prompt is not well-defined or lacks clarity, the AI may interpret it in various ways, leading to inconsistent or off-target responses. This is especially true when the prompt involves open-ended questions or requires the model to make inferences.

When designing prompts, it is crucial to be as specific as possible to guide the model toward the type of response you are looking for. Providing clear instructions, setting expectations, and minimizing room for interpretation can help mitigate inconsistencies.

Example:

Consider a prompt like, "Tell me about space exploration." This is a broad and vague prompt, and the AI could generate responses that range from the history of space exploration to detailed scientific explanations or even opinions about future space travel. However, if you modify the prompt to say, "Explain the history of space exploration and mention the first human mission to the Moon," you are guiding the model toward a more focused and specific response.

Data and Training Bias

AI models are trained on large datasets that reflect the information available on the internet. These datasets are vast and diverse but can also contain inconsistencies, biases, and inaccuracies. When models are trained on biased or incomplete data, the responses they generate can be inconsistent with reality or with the standards you expect.

For example, if the training data includes conflicting information or if certain perspectives are underrepresented, the AI might generate responses that reflect these discrepancies. This can lead to biased or inconsistent outputs, especially when the AI is asked to provide opinions or make judgments.

Example:

If an AI model is trained on a dataset with a predominance of Western media, its responses to cultural or historical questions might not accurately reflect the perspectives of non-Western societies. In this case, the model's inconsistency in handling diverse viewpoints could be a significant challenge.

Strategies to Overcome Model Inconsistencies

To manage and overcome model inconsistencies effectively, there are several strategies that you can implement.

1. Fine-Tuning the Model

Fine-tuning is a process that involves training the AI model on more specific or customized datasets that are aligned with the desired outcomes. By providing the model with a curated set of data that addresses specific domains, you can reduce inconsistencies and guide the AI to produce more relevant and consistent responses.

Fine-tuning may involve providing the model with examples of the type of output you expect or adjusting parameters to ensure the model produces coherent and consistent responses over time.

Example:

If you are using an AI model to assist with legal research, fine-tuning the model with a specialized dataset of legal texts will help it provide more accurate and consistent responses within that domain.

2. Rephrasing and Repeating Prompts

If you notice inconsistencies in the AI's output, try rephrasing your prompt or repeating it multiple times. Small changes in phrasing can sometimes help the model understand your request more clearly and generate more consistent results.

You can also experiment with providing additional context or specifying more details in your prompt. If the AI consistently produces incorrect or inconsistent answers, revisiting the structure of your prompt can be a simple but effective solution.

Example:

If the model fails to provide consistent answers to a question about a historical event, you can try breaking the question down into smaller, more specific parts. Instead of asking, "What happened during the French Revolution?" you might ask, "Who were the key leaders of the French Revolution?" followed by "What were the main causes of the French Revolution?"

3. Using System Instructions

Another strategy is to use system instructions or role-based prompts to guide the AI's behavior. By setting clear parameters for the model, you can help ensure that it remains consistent in how it responds. This is especially useful when you want the model to adopt a specific perspective or act in a particular way.

For example, you can instruct the AI to respond with more formal language, or to take on the role of an expert in a specific field. By defining these roles, you can help the model generate responses that are more aligned with your expectations and reduce inconsistency.

Example:

You could instruct the AI by saying, "You are an expert in ancient history. Please summarize the key events of the Roman Empire." This will help focus the AI's response and ensure it adheres to a specific role, leading to more consistent outputs.

In summary, overcoming model inconsistencies is an ongoing challenge that requires a combination of thoughtful prompt design, fine-tuning, and iterative testing. By understanding the root causes of inconsistencies—such as variability in responses, loss of context, ambiguity, and bias—you can refine your approach and guide AI models to produce more reliable, coherent, and accurate outputs. With the right strategies in place, you can overcome these inconsistencies and unlock the full potential of AI in a wide range of applications.

TROUBLESHOOTING UNEXPECTED OUTPUTS

When working with AI, especially in the realm of prompt engineering, one of the most common challenges you'll face is dealing with unexpected outputs. Despite AI's advanced capabilities, it is far from perfect, and at times, the results can be puzzling, nonsensical, or just plain off-target. Understanding how to troubleshoot these issues is key to improving your AI interactions and ensuring that the outputs you receive align with your expectations. In this section, we will explore practical strategies to handle and correct unexpected results, and offer insights into why they happen in the first place.

1. Identifying the Root Cause of Unexpected Outputs

The first step in troubleshooting is to understand *why* you're getting an unexpected result. AI outputs can be surprising for a range of reasons—sometimes the issue lies with the prompt, sometimes with the model itself, or sometimes with external factors like the data it's been trained on. Here are some of the most common causes of unexpected outputs:

a. Ambiguous or Vague Prompts

If your prompt lacks clarity or specificity, the AI model might generate an answer that seems unrelated or irrelevant to what you were expecting. For example, asking a model to "talk about technology" without further context could lead to a wide range of responses, some of which may feel completely off-topic.

Example:

Prompt: "Tell me about technology." Possible AI Output: "Technology is the use of tools, machines, and systems to make life easier. It has been evolving for centuries with the introduction of the wheel and the steam engine."

In this case, while the response is not incorrect, it might not be the type of "technology" the user had in mind. The vagueness of the prompt led to an overly broad, generic response.

b. Misinterpretation of Context

AI models are good at picking up on patterns, but they don't always follow context in the same way humans do. This can lead to unexpected results when the model "loses track" of the conversational context or misinterprets it.

Example:

If you're having a conversation with the AI and you shift topics without explicitly signaling the change, the model may continue referencing previous ideas, producing responses that seem disconnected from your new line of questioning.

Prompt: "What's the capital of Japan?" Follow-up Prompt: "What is the weather there today?" Expected Output: The weather in Japan today is... Unexpected Output: Tokyo is a bustling city with a lot of culture and history...

In this case, the model doesn't grasp that you've changed the subject and continues discussing Tokyo's features rather than addressing the weather.

c. Model's Randomness or Probabilistic Nature

AI models, particularly those based on deep learning (like GPT), rely on probability to generate responses. While this helps create dynamic, creative outputs, it can also introduce randomness that leads to unexpected answers, even when the prompt is clear. Factors like temperature settings (which control randomness) or sampling methods can lead to results that are unexpected, but still technically valid.

Example:

Prompt: "Explain the law of gravity." AI Output 1: "The law of gravity, discovered by Sir Isaac Newton, explains how objects with mass attract each other." AI Output 2: "Gravity pulls objects toward the Earth and can cause objects to fall from great heights."

Though both answers are valid, they differ in focus and tone. The second response might seem overly simplistic if you were looking for a more scientific explanation, highlighting the randomness factor.

2. Fine-Tuning Your Prompts

Once you've identified that an unexpected output stems from an unclear prompt or context misalignment, the next step is refining your input to guide the model more effectively. Writing precise and targeted prompts can drastically improve the relevance and coherence of the output. Here are some strategies:

a. Increase Specificity

The more specific your prompt, the less room there is for interpretation. Be clear about what you expect in the answer—whether it's the tone, level of detail, or type of information. If the AI doesn't seem to understand the level of complexity you need, adjust your prompt to include instructions on that.

Example:

Instead of: "Tell me about space travel." Try: "Explain the history of human space travel, focusing on the Apollo missions."

The more focused the prompt, the more likely the AI will produce a relevant and accurate output.

b. Provide Clear Context

Provide the AI with enough context to work with, especially in conversations that span multiple turns or involve complex questions. If you notice that the AI is consistently going off-track, consider adding context to clarify your request.

Example:

If you're asking about a movie, you might add: "Give me a review of the movie *Inception* in the style of a film critic." This ensures the AI understands both the subject matter and the tone you're looking for.

c. Set Expectations for the Output

Sometimes the model will output something unexpected simply because it didn't understand your expectations clearly. You can mitigate this by specifying what you want in the answer. For instance, if you want a summary, state it explicitly, and if you need a step-by-step explanation, make that clear too.

Example:

Instead of: "How does photosynthesis work?" Try: "Provide a detailed, step-by-step explanation of how photosynthesis works in plants."

This ensures that the AI focuses on structure and depth.

3. Refining Your AI Parameters

AI models have adjustable parameters that influence how they generate responses. These include things like "temperature" (which controls randomness), "top_p" (which influences how many possible responses the model considers), and "max tokens" (which limits the length of the output). By adjusting these parameters, you can sometimes reduce unexpected results.

a. Controlling Temperature

As we saw in Chapter 6, lowering the temperature (e.g., 0.2 to 0.5) can make the AI more deterministic, reducing randomness in its responses. Higher temperatures (0.7 to 1.0) allow for more creative, diverse answers, but at the cost of greater unpredictability.

Example:

If you are receiving too many irrelevant or creative responses that aren't helpful, consider lowering the temperature to get more straightforward answers.

b. Limiting Output Length

If the AI is generating outputs that are too long or tangential, reducing the "max tokens" limit can ensure the model stays concise and focused.

4. Iterative Testing and Feedback

Even after refining your prompt and adjusting parameters, it may still take some trial and error to get the desired output. Iterative testing involves running the same prompt several times, adjusting the phrasing or parameters each time based on the results you receive. Over time, you'll develop a better understanding of how to craft prompts that lead to consistent and expected outputs.

Example:

You might first test a broad prompt like "Explain quantum mechanics," then, based on the output, adjust your prompt to something more focused like "Explain quantum mechanics in simple terms for high school students." After several iterations, you'll gain insight into how the AI interprets different kinds of input.

5. Handling Outliers and Nonsensical Responses

Sometimes, even after refining your prompt, you may still receive completely nonsensical or irrelevant outputs. This could be due to limitations in the model's training data or simply a random error. When this happens, it's important to approach the output critically and question whether it aligns with your intended outcome. In some cases, you may need to ignore the output and try again, but in others, it might require adjusting the prompt further or even re-training the model for a more specific application.

Example:

If you ask a model, "What is the capital of France?" and it responds with something like "Bananas are rich in potassium," it's likely a case of the model generating a completely irrelevant answer. In such situations, try rephrasing or simplifying the prompt, or using system instructions to correct its behavior.

Troubleshooting unexpected outputs, as previously discussed, involves refining prompts, adjusting parameters, and continuous testing to guide AI effectively.

CHAPTER 12: THE FUTURE OF PROMPT ENGINEERING

The field of prompt engineering is evolving rapidly, and the future holds exciting possibilities. As AI models continue to innovate and become more sophisticated, the demand for skilled prompt engineers is growing. In this chapter, we'll explore the latest advancements in AI technology, examine the increasing need for expertise in prompt crafting, and discuss how you can stay ahead in this dynamic field. Whether you're just starting out or looking to deepen your expertise, understanding the trajectory of AI and prompt engineering will equip you for success in the years to come.

INNOVATIONS IN AI MODELS

As AI continues to evolve, the innovations in AI models are transforming the landscape of prompt engineering. From more sophisticated natural language processing to multimodal capabilities, the advancements in AI models are allowing us to interact with technology in ways we could have only imagined a few years ago.

One of the most significant innovations in recent years has been the improvement in large language models (LLMs). These models, such as GPT-3 and GPT-4, have made remarkable strides in their ability to understand and generate human-like text. They are trained on vast amounts of data, which allows them to provide highly contextualized responses to prompts, offering richer and more nuanced answers than ever before. For example, a model like GPT-4 can understand not just simple commands but can also handle complex instructions with a high degree of coherence, making it invaluable for creative, research, and business applications.

However, innovation in AI models is not limited to language processing alone. Multimodal models, like OpenAI's CLIP, combine the understanding of both images and text. This means that AI can now analyze, interpret, and generate content that is both visual and textual. This opens up entirely new possibilities in fields such as content creation, design, and even accessibility for the visually impaired, where AI can generate both descriptive text and images from a single input prompt.

Furthermore, specialized models are being developed to handle specific tasks with even greater precision. For instance, we now have models dedicated to programming (like GitHub Copilot) that are trained specifically to understand and generate code. These models are tailored to their specific domains, allowing them to achieve higher accuracy and utility than more general models. Similarly, AI in medical research is evolving with models that specialize in analyzing genetic data or imaging results, demonstrating how domain-specific models are pushing the boundaries of what AI can accomplish.

Another area of innovation is reinforcement learning (RL). Traditionally used in training models for games and robotics, RL is now being applied to more complex, real-world scenarios. For example, AI is being used in dynamic environments, like stock market prediction or climate modeling, where it learns from interactions and constantly adapts its approach to improve outcomes over time. These innovations enable AI to handle uncertainty and complexity in ways that were previously unimaginable.

As AI models continue to evolve, prompt engineers will face new challenges and opportunities. For instance, the introduction of multimodal models means that prompts will no longer be confined to just text-based inputs. Engineers will need to craft prompts that account for both textual and visual data, a skill set that will require a deeper understanding of how AI models process different types of information. Similarly, as AI models become more specialized, prompt engineering will require a more tailored approach to align with the specific needs of the domain.

The constant innovation in AI models is creating a dynamic environment for prompt engineers. Staying on top of these innovations and understanding the strengths and limitations of each new model is essential for crafting effective prompts. As AI capabilities expand, so too will the potential of prompt engineering, pushing the boundaries of creativity, productivity, and problem-solving. Keeping an eye on emerging technologies, experimenting with new models, and continuously refining your prompt engineering skills will ensure you remain at the forefront of this exciting field.

THE GROWING DEMAND FOR PROMPT ENGINEERS

As AI technology continues to make significant strides, the demand for prompt engineers is experiencing rapid growth. This specialized role, once niche, is becoming an essential part of the AI ecosystem, especially as AI models become increasingly powerful and widely adopted across various industries. Understanding why this demand is growing—and what it entails—can help you not only appreciate the importance of prompt engineering but also how to position yourself for success in this field.

A New Role in the Age of AI

Prompt engineering is a relatively new field, but it has emerged as a crucial function in bridging the gap between raw AI capabilities and their real-world applications. AI models, like GPT, are incredibly powerful, but they require careful input design to generate meaningful, relevant, and coherent outputs. Without well-crafted prompts, even the most sophisticated AI systems can produce results that are vague, irrelevant, or inaccurate. This is where prompt engineers come in—working as the intermediaries between AI systems and end-users, guiding these models to produce the most effective and impactful responses.

Rising Demand Across Industries

The demand for prompt engineers is not confined to one particular industry; it spans multiple sectors, all of which have recognized the need for effective AI implementation. From content creation to software development, healthcare, marketing, and finance, AI is increasingly being integrated into core business operations, driving the need for experts who can craft precise, context-aware prompts.

- **Content Creation**: As businesses and creators leverage AI for content generation—whether it's blog posts, social media content, or video scripts—the ability to prompt AI models to produce high-quality, engaging material is crucial. This requires a deep understanding of language, creativity, and the nuances of AI's capabilities. Prompt engineers who can guide AI to produce well-targeted content are in high demand.

- **Software Development**: In coding and debugging, AI tools such as GitHub Copilot are transforming how developers approach coding. However, crafting the right prompts to ensure these tools provide useful and relevant code requires specialized skills. Prompt engineers are crucial in optimizing AI's effectiveness in these contexts, reducing errors and enhancing development speed.

- **Customer Support**: AI-powered chatbots and virtual assistants are being used across industries to improve customer service and streamline operations. These systems require finely-tuned prompts to ensure they understand and address customer queries accurately. Prompt engineers play a vital role in shaping these conversations, making them both efficient and natural.

- **Healthcare**: AI's role in healthcare, from medical diagnoses to drug discovery, is expanding rapidly. However, working with AI in such a high-stakes field requires precision and an understanding of both the medical domain and AI's capabilities. Prompt engineers working in healthcare must be able to craft prompts that help AI deliver accurate and reliable results, while also considering ethical guidelines and data privacy.

Why the Demand is Growing

There are several factors contributing to the growing demand for prompt engineers.

1. **Complexity of AI Models**: As AI models become more advanced, they also become more complex. The output from these models is heavily influenced by the input prompts, and small changes to the phrasing or structure of a prompt can have a significant impact on the results.

As AI models scale in complexity, so does the need for specialized professionals who can tailor inputs to generate the most effective outputs.

2. **AI Adoption Across Industries**: As more industries begin to realize the benefits of AI, there is an increasing need for experts who can guide AI toward specific business goals. Companies are investing in AI to streamline operations, improve customer experiences, and drive innovation. The growing integration of AI into various workflows has created a surge in the demand for prompt engineers to help companies leverage these tools effectively.

3. **Optimization of AI for Real-World Applications**: While AI models are powerful, they often require fine-tuning to perform well in real-world scenarios. The task of guiding AI to deliver optimal results is not a one-size-fits-all process. Prompt engineers must understand the context and nuances of the specific task to craft prompts that maximize the potential of the AI, making this skill set increasingly sought after.

Skills Required to Meet the Growing Demand

With the rising demand for prompt engineers comes the need for a specific set of skills that blend technical knowledge with creativity and communication. Here's a closer look at some of the essential skills needed for the role:

- **Understanding of AI and Machine Learning**: A solid understanding of how AI and machine learning models work is crucial. While you don't need to be an AI researcher, having a grasp of model behavior, data processing, and algorithms will help you craft more effective prompts.

- **Language and Communication Skills**: Since prompts are typically text-based, strong language and communication skills are a must. You'll need to understand how to phrase inputs to convey the desired outcome, and sometimes this requires creative thinking and adaptability.

- **Problem-Solving**: AI models can produce unexpected outputs, and part of the prompt engineer's job is to troubleshoot these results and adjust prompts to achieve the right output. This requires a strong problem-solving mindset.

- **Domain Expertise**: Depending on the industry you're working in, domain-specific knowledge can be incredibly helpful. For example, if you're working in healthcare, understanding medical terminology and context is essential for crafting prompts that lead to accurate and actionable results.

- **Ethical Awareness**: With AI's increasing influence on decision-making, an understanding of ethical considerations—such as fairness, bias, and privacy—is essential. As a prompt engineer, you'll need to ensure that the prompts you design lead to responsible and unbiased outputs.

Preparing for the Future

Given the demand for prompt engineers, it's clear that this is a role with long-term potential. However, staying ahead in the field requires ongoing learning and adaptation. As AI technology evolves, new tools, models, and techniques will emerge. To stay relevant, prompt engineers must be proactive about their professional development, keeping up with the latest advancements in AI research, experimenting with new models, and refining their prompt engineering skills.

In addition, there is increasing emphasis on collaboration between AI practitioners and domain experts. By working closely with professionals in fields like healthcare, education, or business, prompt engineers can ensure that AI tools are used effectively and ethically in those specific contexts.

The role of the prompt engineer is becoming indispensable in today's AI-driven world. As AI continues to infiltrate more industries, the need for experts who can understand, guide, and optimize AI output will only continue to grow. Whether you're just starting out or you've been in the field for some time, positioning yourself as a prompt engineering expert will open up a world of opportunities. The future of AI is bright, and as a prompt engineer, you will be at the forefront, shaping how AI interacts with the world.

HOW TO STAY AHEAD IN THE FIELD

In the world of AI and prompt engineering, evolution is fast and constant. To remain competitive, adopting a continuous learning approach is essential. As technologies develop, new techniques, tools, and methodologies emerge, and staying updated on these changes is crucial.

The first step is following the latest research and developments in AI technologies. Subscribing to academic journals, attending conferences and webinars, and reading articles from experts in the field are excellent ways to stay informed. Online communities, such as forums and discussion groups, are valuable resources for sharing knowledge and asking questions.

Additionally, experimenting with new AI models and prompt engineering tools is key. Hands-on experience is one of the best ways to refine your skills and discover new techniques. Using platforms that provide access to advanced AI models like GPT or similar models allows you to explore features and test various interaction modes.

Another crucial aspect is developing an analytical mindset. Understanding how AI models make decisions and optimizing prompts for more accurate results is a highly sought-after skill. Reflecting on how each prompt can be fine-tuned, testing different approaches, and consistently analyzing results allows for continuous improvement.

Engaging with the broader AI and prompt engineering community is also valuable. Contributing to open-source projects, writing blog posts, or participating in online forums and Q&A platforms can help solidify your understanding and reputation. Sharing your experiences and solutions to challenges not only strengthens your own knowledge but also fosters connections with professionals in the industry.

Lastly, never underestimate the importance of soft skills. Clear and effective communication with multidisciplinary teams, managing client expectations, and explaining complex concepts in simple terms are abilities that should never be overlooked.

Keeping up with technological advancements and continuously improving your skills will allow you to meet the challenges of the field and leverage them to your advantage.

RESOURCES AND PRACTICE

CHAPTER 13: TOOLS FOR PROMPT ENGINEERS

As prompt engineers, having the right tools at your disposal can make all the difference in the quality and efficiency of your work. In this chapter, we'll explore the various AI platforms and software available to streamline and enhance your prompt engineering process. From popular platforms like OpenAI and MidJourney, which provide powerful AI models, to specialized plugins and optimization tools, you'll learn how to select the best resources for your needs. Whether you're looking to fine-tune your prompts or experiment with different models, understanding these tools is essential for mastering the art of prompt engineering.

POPULAR AI PLATFORMS (OPENAI, MIDJOURNEY, ETC.)

When it comes to AI prompt engineering, selecting the right platform is crucial. Different platforms come with their own strengths, capabilities, and unique features that can help streamline your workflow, improve results, and expand the scope of what you can achieve. Let's take a look at some of the most popular AI platforms available today, starting with OpenAI and MidJourney.

OpenAI: A Robust and Versatile Platform

OpenAI has quickly established itself as a leader in the AI field, providing some of the most advanced and widely used models for prompt engineering. Their models, such as GPT-3 and GPT-4, are designed to handle a wide range of natural language processing tasks, from generating human-like text to creating coherent, context-aware dialogues.

Key Strengths of OpenAI:

1. **Scalability:** OpenAI offers various API access options that allow you to scale up or down depending on your project's needs. Whether you need a single response or millions of queries, OpenAI can accommodate a variety of demands.

2. **Versatility in Application:** Whether you're working on creative writing, technical explanations, data analysis, or even code generation, OpenAI's models are capable of performing across a multitude of domains. The models are especially strong in generating conversational responses, making them ideal for applications like chatbots, customer service automation, and content creation.

3. **Customizability:** OpenAI allows users to fine-tune their models on specific datasets or modify responses using specific instructions or temperature settings. This is particularly helpful for prompt engineers looking to optimize model outputs for highly specific or niche tasks.

Example in Practice: Imagine you're building a customer service chatbot. OpenAI's GPT models can be tailored to answer queries based on your company's product catalog, customer feedback, and frequently asked questions. Fine-tuning the model using your specific dataset would result in a chatbot that responds in a highly accurate and context-aware manner.

MidJourney: Pushing the Boundaries of Visual Creativity

MidJourney is another powerful platform, but with a focus on generative art rather than text. If your work as a prompt engineer involves more creative output, such as image generation or visual content, MidJourney could be the platform you turn to. With its robust AI capabilities, MidJourney allows you to create high-quality visuals from simple text prompts.

Key Strengths of MidJourney:

1. **Creative and Artistic Focus:** Unlike other AI platforms, MidJourney specializes in turning text descriptions into stunning, often surreal, pieces of art. If you're working in creative fields like graphic design, advertising, or digital art, MidJourney opens up new possibilities for generating unique visuals on demand.

2. **Interactivity and Feedback:** One of the platform's standout features is its interactive approach. You can generate initial images, then refine and tweak them by adding more detailed prompts or adjusting parameters based on the output. This iterative feedback process helps guide the model towards a result that matches your vision.

3. **Community and Collaboration:** MidJourney also stands out for its active online community, which shares ideas, techniques, and tips. This is particularly helpful when you're just starting out or when you're stuck and need inspiration or suggestions for refining your prompts.

Example in Practice: Suppose you're a game designer creating an immersive fantasy world. With MidJourney, you can input prompts like "a futuristic city on Mars at sunset with neon lights reflecting on glass buildings" and the AI will generate a visual representation of that scene. You can tweak the prompt further to refine the details, adding additional elements like characters or specific lighting effects, and generate multiple iterations until you get the perfect image.

Other Platforms to Explore

While OpenAI and MidJourney are two of the most popular platforms, there are several others worth exploring depending on your needs:

1. **Google's AI (BERT, LaMDA):** Known for its conversational abilities, Google's AI models are frequently used for developing chatbots, search engine optimizations, and other language-based applications. LaMDA, in particular, is designed to have more natural and open-ended conversations.

2. **Anthropic's Claude:** Anthropic offers Claude, an AI assistant designed with safety and ethical considerations in mind. It emphasizes reducing harmful outputs while maximizing the ability to understand complex prompts and provide coherent, fact-based responses.

3. **Hugging Face:** Hugging Face provides an open-source platform for machine learning and natural language processing. It has a wide range of pre-trained models, making it an excellent choice for developers looking to experiment with different algorithms and build custom AI solutions.

4. **Runway:** Runway is a creative AI platform that combines visual arts and machine learning. It allows prompt engineers to generate everything from video editing tools to AI-generated animations, making it a versatile option for creative professionals.

Selecting the Right Platform for You

Choosing the right AI platform depends largely on the type of project you're working on. Are you focused on generating text, or are you working in a more creative field that involves images and video? Do you need a platform with powerful customization options, or are you looking for something more out-of-the-box?

In general, OpenAI is a great option for a wide variety of applications involving language and dialogue, while MidJourney excels in creative visual arts. The key is understanding what you need from your platform and then selecting the tool that can best meet those demands.

By utilizing the strengths of these platforms, prompt engineers can significantly enhance the quality and efficiency of their work. Whether you're generating text, designing visuals, or creating complex models, these platforms are equipped to help you achieve high-level results with precision and ease.

Remember that artificial intelligence continues to evolve; staying up-to-date on new platforms, models, and advances is essential for rapid engineers. By continually exploring new tools, you ensure that you take advantage of the best available technologies, keep your skills sharp, and remain at the forefront of the field, as discussed in the previous chapter.

SOFTWARE AND PLUGINS FOR PROMPT OPTIMIZATION

When it comes to optimizing your prompts, there are several software tools and plugins available that can enhance both your efficiency and the quality of your results. As a prompt engineer, having the right tools in your workflow can make all the difference. These tools help you experiment with different approaches, refine your inputs, and ensure that your prompts yield more accurate, relevant, and creative outputs.

Prompt Engineering Software

There are specific platforms and applications dedicated to helping you craft, test, and optimize prompts. These often come with built-in features that suggest improvements based on the intended outcome. One such example is **FlowGPT,** which is a prompt generator and optimization tool that can suggest edits to your input based on the context and the model's expected response. This kind of software can be a massive time-saver, especially when working with large-scale projects that require a fine-tuned approach.

Similarly, **AI Dungeon** offers a creative writing platform where users can experiment with narrative prompts. It's not just for entertainment—this platform also helps users understand the nuances of prompt building, which can be applied to more practical use cases like customer support or data analysis. Being able to quickly test and modify your prompts within a controlled environment allows you to learn and improve much faster.

Plugins for Integrating AI into Workflows

In addition to standalone software, there are many plugins available for popular platforms, which allow for the seamless integration of AI models into your workflow. For instance, **GPT-3 plugins for WordPress** can automate content creation for blogs, articles, and even product descriptions. These plugins can analyze your content and automatically generate suggestions for new prompts based on the style, tone, and keywords you're targeting.

This feature can be particularly useful for those working in digital marketing, where continuous content generation is crucial.

Another highly useful plugin is **ChatGPT for Slack**, which integrates the power of AI directly into your team's communication platform. This allows for real-time query resolution and task automation. Whether it's generating responses for customer support or drafting up answers for FAQs, these plugins save time and streamline operations. The ability to trigger AI responses within your usual workflow makes the process much more efficient.

Optimization Tools

While AI is powerful, the key to effective prompt engineering lies in the ability to optimize the input for the desired output. This is where advanced tools come in. One example is **PromptPerfect**, a tool designed to help users optimize their prompts based on desired output. PromptPerfect analyses your input, suggests improvements, and predicts the model's behavior, making it easier for prompt engineers to refine their queries and obtain more precise answers.

Replit is another tool that supports AI-assisted programming. If you're working on coding-related prompts, this platform can automatically suggest code optimizations, analyze input for potential errors, and help you fine-tune your commands. Its collaboration features also enable you to work with other developers, providing opportunities to learn from peers and incorporate best practices.

AI Model Tuning Software

Some software tools focus on fine-tuning existing models to better suit specific use cases. Fine-tuning is the process of adjusting a pre-trained model with additional data to make it more accurate or aligned with the specific needs of the task. For instance, **OpenAI's API** allows developers to fine-tune their own versions of the GPT model to create highly specialized applications. This is a powerful way to ensure that your prompts interact with the model in the way you intend, reducing ambiguity and improving the quality of the outputs.

Weights & Biases is another tool that can be extremely valuable in this context. It helps in tracking experiments, visualizing results, and managing different versions of models. By keeping track of what works best for your prompt engineering needs, you can apply the right strategies to your inputs and further optimize the results.

Version Control for Prompts

As you create and test various prompts, keeping track of which ones work best for specific tasks is vital. Software like **Git** and **GitHub** can be incredibly useful in this respect. While they're commonly used for coding, these tools can also manage versions of your prompts and experiments, making it easier to keep track of changes and ensure that you always have access to the most effective prompt variations. You can store multiple versions, experiment with different inputs, and document which prompts resulted in the most useful AI outputs.

6. AI-Enhanced Writing Assistants

For those working with text-based prompts, AI-powered writing assistants like **Grammarly** and **Hemingway Editor** can be useful for improving prompt clarity and structure. These tools not only check for grammar and style but also suggest ways to simplify or make prompts more direct and efficient. By enhancing the quality of your language, these tools ensure that the AI better understands your intent and produces more refined responses.

In summary, optimizing prompts is a crucial aspect of becoming an effective prompt engineer, and using the right software and plugins can drastically improve your results. Whether you're refining your prompt construction through testing, enhancing content generation with plugins, or fine-tuning models for specialized tasks, these tools enable you to produce high-quality outputs with greater efficiency. As AI continues to evolve, so too will the tools available for prompt engineers, making it essential for you to stay updated and adaptable in your approach.

CHAPTER 14: PRACTICE MAKES PERFECT

In this chapter, we'll dive into practical exercises designed to sharpen your prompt engineering skills. Whether you're just starting out or looking to test your expertise, these step-by-step exercises will guide you through the process of creating effective prompts. You'll encounter both beginner-friendly tasks and more advanced scenarios, each carefully crafted to help you understand the intricacies of AI interactions. We'll also explore real-world examples and case studies, offering insights into how prompt engineering is applied in various industries. By the end of this chapter, you'll be better equipped to apply your skills confidently in any situation

STEP-BY-STEP PROMPT ENGINEERING EXERCISES

1. Factual Question Exercise

Objective: Learn to ask direct questions and get concise, correct answers.

Exercise: Start with a simple, direct question:

Prompt: *"What is the capital of France?"*

Result: *"The capital of France is Paris."*

Advanced Exercise: Now, let's make the prompt more detailed and specific: Prompt: "What is the capital of France and what are some famous landmarks there? Limit your response to 150 characters."

Result: *"The capital of France is Paris. Famous landmarks include the Eiffel Tower, Louvre, and Notre-Dame Cathedral."*

Notice how adding the character limit narrows the response, making it more concise. You can also specify the tone or style of the response. For example, if you want a formal tone, you can specify:

Prompt: *"What is the capital of France and what are some famous landmarks? Provide a formal response in 150 characters."*

Result: *"The capital of France is Paris, home to landmarks such as the Eiffel Tower, the Louvre, and the Notre-Dame Cathedral."*

This allows you to control the length, tone, and style of the response.

2. Task-Oriented Prompt Exercise

Objective: Guide the AI toward a specific task.

Exercise: If you ask an AI to generate a list of ideas, the generic prompt might look like this:

Prompt: *"Give me ways to improve productivity."*

Result: *"1. Time management. 2. Reduce distractions. 3. Use productivity tools."*

Advanced Exercise: Now, refine the request to a specific field or style, and set expectations for the format:

Prompt: *"Give me ways to improve productivity for a team of software engineers working remotely. Provide a concise list of five tips in bullet points."*

Result: *"1. Use agile frameworks like Scrum for task management. 2. Set daily stand-up meetings to track progress. 3. Use Slack for team communication. 4. Create clear goals and expectations. 5. Use cloud-based collaboration tools."*

You can also set the tone or perspective by specifying that the AI should "act as an expert in productivity for remote teams," which helps to tailor the response more effectively to your needs.

3. Creative Writing Exercise

Objective: Use the AI to create original stories or content.

Exercise:Start with a simple request for a short story:

Prompt: *"Write a short story about a scientist who invents time travel."*

Result: *"Dr. Eva Hughes, a renowned physicist, was working late one evening in her lab when she accidentally activated the prototype time machine. She found herself transported to ancient Egypt, where she met Cleopatra and witnessed the building of the Great Pyramid."*

Advanced Exercise: Now, ask for a more refined story with a particular style and tone:

Prompt: *"Write a suspenseful short story about a scientist who invents time travel. The tone should be dark and mysterious, with a cliffhanger ending."*

Result: *"Dr. Hughes activated the time machine with trembling hands, unsure of what awaited her. She stepped into the swirling vortex, only to find herself in a desolate, post-apocalyptic future. Before she could make sense of her surroundings, a shadow loomed in the distance. It was too late to return."*

Notice how the addition of a tone and a cliffhanger ending shaped the direction of the story, demonstrating how specific instructions can result in a more nuanced outcome.

4. Instructional Prompt Exercise

Objective: Use the AI to explain complex concepts in simple terms.

Exercise: Start with a basic explanation:

Prompt: *"Explain how photosynthesis works."*

Result: *"Photosynthesis is the process by which plants convert light energy into chemical energy. Plants use sunlight, water, and carbon dioxide to produce glucose and oxygen. This process occurs mainly in the chloroplasts of plant cells."*

Advanced Exercise: Specify the target audience and tone for clarity:

Prompt: *"Explain how photosynthesis works in simple terms for a 10-year-old. Keep it light and fun."*

Result: *"Photosynthesis is like a recipe that plants use to make their food! They mix sunlight, water, and air, and—voilà!—they get their energy. Plus, they give us oxygen to breathe!"*

Now the AI adapts to a more playful tone, making the explanation accessible for younger audiences.

Advanced Exercise with Expert Persona:

Prompt: *"Explain how photosynthesis works as if you are a biologist giving a lecture. Use formal language and explain the process in depth."*

Result: *"Photosynthesis is a biochemical process in which light energy is captured by chlorophyll and used to convert carbon dioxide and water into glucose, which serves as the plant's primary source of energy. This process occurs in the chloroplasts and produces oxygen as a byproduct."*

By asking the AI to take on the role of an expert, it provides a more formal, detailed response.

5. Comparative Prompt Exercise

Objective: Make the AI compare two concepts or entities.

Exercise:Ask for a generic comparison:

Prompt: *"Compare apples and oranges."*

Result: *"Apples and oranges are both fruits, but apples are typically sweet and crunchy, while oranges are juicy and tangy."*

Advanced Exercise: Now, ask for a detailed comparison with a set of guidelines and tone:

Prompt: *"Compare apples and oranges in terms of nutritional value, taste, and health benefits. Provide a formal comparison with at least three key points."*

Result: *"1. Nutritional Value: Apples are rich in fiber, while oranges contain high levels of vitamin C. 2. Taste: Apples are typically sweet with a crisp texture, while oranges have a tangy, juicy flavor. 3. Health Benefits: Apples support digestion and cardiovascular health, while oranges boost the immune system and prevent colds."*

Adding specific instructions on the format and tone of the comparison refines the output, giving you more comprehensive information.

6. Scenario-based Prompt Exercise

Objective: Test how the AI responds to a specific scenario and ask for a refined, professional output.

Exercise: Start with a basic prompt asking for information on a hypothetical discovery:

Prompt: *"Write a news article about the discovery of a new dinosaur skeleton never found before."*

Result: *"Scientists have recently uncovered an astonishing new dinosaur skeleton in the remote hills of Montana. The discovery, which dates back over 70 million years, sheds light on previously unknown species. Researchers are eager to analyze the fossil to better understand the ancient ecosystem."*

Advanced Exercise: Now, refine the prompt with detailed instructions and a specified format:

Prompt: *"Write a formal, professional news article about the discovery of a new dinosaur skeleton never found before. Act as an expert journalist. The article should be no longer than 500 words, avoid repetition, and maintain a neutral tone throughout, without addressing the readers directly."*

Result: *"In an unprecedented archaeological breakthrough, paleontologists have uncovered a new dinosaur skeleton in the hills of Montana, marking the first-ever discovery of this species.*

The well-preserved fossil, believed to be over 70 million years old, offers valuable insights into the ecosystem of the late Cretaceous period. Experts have identified key features that distinguish this new species from known dinosaurs, including its unique bone structure and distinct physical traits. The team of researchers, led by Dr. Emily Zhang, believes that this discovery will significantly expand our understanding of prehistoric life. Initial analyzes suggest that the dinosaur was a herbivore, with a diet that likely consisted of dense plant matter from the region's rich flora. The fossil is expected to provide further clues into the environment in which these creatures lived, particularly in relation to the climate and vegetation during the Cretaceous period. While the discovery is still in the early stages of study, paleontologists are hopeful that continued excavation and research will yield even more significant findings in the coming months."

In this advanced prompt, by asking the AI to "act as an expert journalist," you receive a more formal, polished response with a professional tone. The character count limitation ensures the article stays concise, and instructions to avoid repetition help eliminate unnecessary details. Additionally, specifying that the article should not address the reader directly ensures a more objective, news-style presentation.

This updated exercise shows how refining your prompt, setting clear expectations, and providing specific guidelines can result in a much more polished, professional output.

MASTERING TEXT-TO-IMAGE AI PROMPTS

Of course, the same principles apply to generative AIs for images and videos, though with different parameters compared to generative text AIs. While text-based AIs focus on processing and creating verbal responses based on prompts, generative AIs for images and videos rely on parameters that influence the visual appearance or dynamics of a scene.

When working with images or videos, the focus shifts to elements such as:

1. **Visual Detail**: Unlike text, where you specify tone, structure, or length, image and video prompts emphasize visual aspects like scene type, dominant color, artistic style, or even camera angles in the case of videos.

2. **Style and Composition**: You can request specific artistic styles for images, such as "surrealism" or "digital art," and adjust parameters for composition, lighting, and object arrangement. For example, a prompt like "create a futuristic landscape with neon colors" involves a different approach than a standard text request.

3. **Animation and Movement**: Video prompts include parameters such as movement speed, animation style (e.g., 2D or 3D), and the fluidity of motion. These dynamic aspects add complexity beyond a simple verbal description, as they involve representing motion over time.

4. **Temporal Context**: In videos, the temporal context is critical. Generative video AIs consider duration, scene sequences, and frame transitions, while image generation typically focuses on a single visual frame.

In summary, while the core principle of tailoring prompts for more precise results applies across text, images, and videos, images and videos require different parameters. These parameters focus on visual, stylistic, and dynamic factors that guide the quality and direction of the generated work.

Additionally, for advanced prompt engineers, there are specialized terms and techniques that refine prompts further, particularly in generative AIs for images and videos. These include:

1. **Semantic Keywords**: Words like "high contrast," "low saturation," or "soft lighting" can influence the mood and atmosphere of the generated image or video, helping to fine-tune the visual feel.

2. **Depth and Perspective**: In advanced image prompts, specifying depth of field, perspective, or even camera focal length can enhance composition. For example, "a close-up of a butterfly with shallow depth of field in soft sunlight" offers more control over focus and composition.

3. **Rendering Techniques**: Certain prompts request specific rendering techniques, such as ray tracing, global illumination, or bokeh effects, to achieve realistic visuals or a particular artistic flair.

4. **Scene Composition**: Experienced prompt engineers often use principles like the rule of thirds or the golden ratio to ensure visual balance and harmony in the image or video.

5. **Temporal Complexity for Videos**: Video prompts may involve parameters like frame rate, motion blur, slow motion, or looping effects, which define how the visual flow evolves over time.

6. **AI Style Transfer**: Advanced users may incorporate phrases like "apply the style of a Van Gogh painting to the scene" or "in the manner of Japanese anime," blending different artistic influences for unique results.

7. **Multi-Object Interactions**: For both images and videos, prompt engineers can include terms like "interaction between elements" to define how objects relate to one another in the scene, such as "a cat playing with a ball of yarn."

The more you practice generating images by experimenting with different prompts (both with MidJourney and other text-to-image generative AIs), the more you learn and become confident in your ability to create precise and compelling visual prompts. With time and experimentation, you'll better understand how AI interprets your instructions and how to refine your prompts for even more sophisticated and specific results.

By mastering these additional levels of detail, prompt engineers can guide generative AI to produce highly nuanced, stylized, and visually sophisticated work, going beyond basic prompts to achieve highly specific and personalized results.

CHAPTER 15: HUMAN-AI COLLABORATION

In this final chapter, we explore the collaborative potential between humans and AI. While AI brings immense power to the table, it is our creativity, intuition, and judgment that can truly unlock its full potential. The future will not be about AI replacing us, but about humans and AI working together to achieve new heights. This chapter will focus on how to build productive and beneficial collaborations with AI models and how human creativity will continue to shape and guide AI in meaningful ways. It's about embracing the fusion of human ingenuity and artificial intelligence

BUILDING EFFECTIVE PARTNERSHIPS WITH AI MODELS

In today's rapidly evolving technological landscape, creating effective partnerships with AI models is not just a luxury—it's a necessity. The idea of collaborating with AI might seem like something out of science fiction, but it's an approach that is now commonplace in multiple industries, from content creation to business analytics, and even healthcare. In this section, we'll dive deep into the process of fostering these partnerships, exploring how AI can become a powerful tool when used in harmony with human creativity, intuition, and expertise.

Understanding the Role of AI as a Partner

To build an effective partnership with AI, it's essential to first understand the role that AI plays in the equation. AI is, by nature, a tool that processes information, analyzes data, and generates outputs based on its programming and input. However, unlike traditional tools, AI can learn and adapt over time. This dynamic characteristic allows it to not only assist with specific tasks but also to enhance your capabilities, offering insights and solutions that may not have been immediately obvious.

For example, when it comes to writing, AI can help you brainstorm ideas, structure your content, or even provide suggestions on how to improve the tone or clarity of your message. However, the true value of the partnership comes when you blend the AI's ability to process vast amounts of data with your own understanding of the context, audience, and nuanced objectives. This symbiotic relationship allows for an output that neither the human nor the AI could have achieved alone.

Effective Communication with AI

One of the most critical aspects of building a successful partnership with AI is understanding how to communicate with it. For many users, especially beginners, interacting with AI can feel like speaking to a black box—input comes in, output comes out, but it's not always clear why the AI produces the results it does. However, with the right approach, you can transform this "black box" into a powerful collaborator.

In the case of text-based AI, like GPT models, the most important factor in communication is the clarity of the prompts you give. A well-crafted prompt can guide the AI to produce outputs that are not only relevant but also aligned with your goals. It's not just about asking the right questions; it's about asking them in the right way. By refining your approach to prompt writing, you ensure that the AI's responses are accurate, coherent, and useful.

When using generative AI for images or video, effective communication takes on an even more nuanced form. For instance, when generating an image through a model like MidJourney, instead of simply requesting "a landscape," you might specify "a serene mountain landscape at sunset, with a misty atmosphere and soft, warm lighting." The more specific your prompt, the more likely the AI will be able to produce an image that matches your vision.

Collaboration in Problem-Solving

AI excels at analyzing data and recognizing patterns, but it lacks the ability to make decisions based on human emotion, ethics, or complex social dynamics. This is where your unique expertise comes into play. The AI is a powerful assistant, but it requires direction and context to be truly effective. It can help you solve problems by offering data-driven insights, but your knowledge of the problem's broader context is crucial for determining the relevance and ethics of the AI's suggestions.

Consider the example of AI in the healthcare industry. AI models can analyze medical data to assist in diagnosing diseases, predicting outcomes, and even recommending treatments. However, these suggestions must be interpreted and contextualized by healthcare professionals who can factor in the patient's individual needs, values, and circumstances. The AI provides the raw data, but it is the healthcare professional who makes the final judgment. This same principle applies across industries, where AI can offer insights, but human judgment and intuition guide decision-making.

Continuous Improvement Through Iteration

Effective partnerships with AI models are built over time. Just like in human relationships, the more you work with AI, the better you'll understand its capabilities and limitations. This iterative process is key to maximizing the value of AI. The AI may not always get things perfect on the first try, but with each iteration, you can refine your prompts, tweak the model's parameters, and improve the results.

For example, if you're using AI to generate content, you might begin by giving the model a general prompt, such as "write a blog post about AI and prompt engineering." As you review the AI's output, you may realize that the tone isn't quite right or that some sections lack depth. You can then adjust your prompt, providing more specific instructions on tone, length, or content, to guide the AI toward a more refined output. Over time, the process becomes more efficient, and the results become more aligned with your expectations.

The Importance of Human Creativity

While AI is powerful in its ability to process information and generate outputs based on patterns, it's your creativity that transforms those outputs into something truly impactful. AI can assist in generating ideas, optimizing workflows, and automating repetitive tasks, but it doesn't have the intrinsic ability to innovate. Creativity, intuition, and emotional intelligence are uniquely human qualities that will continue to drive the most meaningful advancements in AI collaboration.

Think about the role of AI in creative fields like art, music, and literature. AI can generate stunning images or write coherent text, but it is human creativity that guides these outputs toward originality and emotional resonance. For instance, an artist might use an AI tool to generate a base image but then apply their own artistic skills to refine and personalize the piece. In the same way, AI can assist with brainstorming ideas, but it is the human mind that shapes those ideas into something uniquely valuable.

Building a Mutually Beneficial Relationship

Ultimately, building an effective partnership with AI models is about creating a mutually beneficial relationship where both you and the AI contribute your strengths. The AI offers powerful tools for analysis, generation, and automation, while you bring context, creativity, and decision-making abilities that guide the AI's outputs toward meaningful and valuable results. By understanding the AI's capabilities, communicating effectively with it, and using your own expertise to guide its outputs, you can unlock the full potential of this collaboration.

In the end, AI is not a replacement for human creativity or expertise—it is a tool that enhances it. By fostering effective partnerships with AI, you not only increase your own capabilities but also contribute to the development of more intelligent, ethical, and creative AI systems for the future. The future of AI is one of collaboration, not competition, and by embracing this mindset, you can harness the power of AI to transform your work, your industry, and the world around you.

THE ROLE OF CREATIVITY IN THE AI-DRIVEN FUTURE

As we step into a future where artificial intelligence is an integral part of daily life, it's easy to focus on the technical aspects—how AI works, what it can do, and how it can help optimize processes. However, amid all the technological advancements, one fundamental human characteristic remains crucial: creativity. In the AI-driven world, creativity isn't just important; it's indispensable. It's the thread that ties together data-driven outputs and meaningful, original work. In this section, we'll explore how creativity will shape the future of AI, particularly in areas like prompt engineering, content generation, art, and problem-solving.

Understanding the Symbiosis Between AI and Creativity

AI models, particularly those that are generative (like GPT for text or MidJourney for images), operate by recognizing patterns in vast datasets. These models can create text, images, and even music by predicting the next likely element in a sequence. They excel at generating responses based on input and learning from patterns, but the creative spark—the ability to come up with truly novel ideas, push boundaries, and inject meaning into something—remains distinctly human. This is where your role as a prompt engineer, creator, or developer becomes vital.

In essence, AI can be a catalyst for creativity, but it relies on you to provide direction. The creativity you bring to the table allows AI to generate outputs that are not just useful or functional, but also inspired and groundbreaking. For example, when creating an art piece using an AI image generator, you don't just give a basic prompt like "a forest." You add layers to it—"a mystical forest with fog and golden sunlight breaking through the trees"—to guide the AI toward something more specific, more vibrant, and more evocative. Without your creative input, the AI would simply generate generic images based on patterns it has learned, which might not be aligned with your vision.

Creativity in Prompt Engineering

In prompt engineering, the role of creativity is central to shaping how AI will respond. It's not just about knowing how to interact with an AI; it's about knowing how to communicate your vision clearly, concisely, and creatively. The more creatively you approach your prompts, the more effectively you can unlock the full potential of an AI model.

Consider the task of writing a story using an AI tool like GPT. If you simply ask the AI to "write a short story," the result might be passable, but it will lack flair, depth, or the personal touch that makes stories resonate with readers. However, by creatively crafting your prompt, such as "Write a short story about a detective in a futuristic city, who solves a crime using only the power of memory," you're able to guide the AI in a way that helps it generate an output that is not only cohesive but also engaging and fresh. Your creativity adds the critical layer of direction, making the result unique rather than generic.

The creativity here also lies in iterating your prompts. Sometimes the first result isn't quite right, and that's where human creativity shines. You can adjust the prompt to refine the output: "Now, make the detective a former psychologist, whose understanding of human behavior allows them to solve crimes in unconventional ways." This back-and-forth process of refining prompts, tweaking details, and iterating is a fundamentally creative act that elevates the AI-generated content into something extraordinary.

Creativity in AI-Assisted Design and Art

In fields like digital art and design, AI is already playing a transformative role. AI models can generate stunning visuals from simple text descriptions, creating everything from abstract designs to lifelike portraits. But, once again, it's the human creator who provides the vital spark of creativity. AI can provide inspiration and ideas, but it is the artist who interprets these ideas, adds context, and applies their unique perspective to the work.

For example, AI-generated images can serve as a starting point for a graphic designer working on a new logo. The designer might feed the AI specific keywords and instructions, and the model will generate several concepts based on those parameters. However, the designer's creativity is what takes those concepts and refines them, experimenting with colors, shapes, and proportions to create a final design that is not only aesthetically pleasing but also aligns with the company's branding and vision. In this way, AI doesn't replace the designer's creativity—it enhances it, offering new possibilities that wouldn't have been considered otherwise.

This kind of collaboration can be seen in the use of AI tools in music production as well. AI can help musicians by generating melodies, harmonies, or even lyrics based on a few input parameters. But, ultimately, the artist's creativity is what transforms those AI-generated pieces into complete compositions that evoke emotion, tell a story, and connect with listeners. The technology becomes a powerful tool in the creative process, expanding what is possible, but the artist's touch remains irreplaceable.

Creativity as a Catalyst for Innovation

As AI continues to evolve, it will increasingly become a tool that amplifies creativity, enabling new forms of innovation across industries. By using AI to automate repetitive tasks or generate initial drafts, creators can free up more time to focus on the aspects of their work that truly require human intuition and inspiration. This leads to more innovative outcomes, as creators are no longer bogged down by the mundane aspects of their tasks and can instead channel their energy into refining and exploring new ideas.

For instance, in the field of architecture, AI is being used to design buildings that are both structurally sound and visually unique. While the AI can help design efficient structures by analyzing building materials, weather patterns, and environmental factors, it's the architect who brings a sense of creativity to the project. They decide how to incorporate natural elements, cultural significance, and artistic vision into the design, resulting in buildings that are both functional and beautiful. In this case, AI acts as a tool that accelerates the design process, but it's the architect's creative thinking that leads to truly innovative results.

The Future of Creativity in AI Collaboration

Looking ahead, the role of creativity in AI is only set to expand. As AI models become more sophisticated, they will provide even greater opportunities for collaboration between humans and machines. But, despite these advancements, one thing remains certain: the human touch will continue to be essential. AI may be able to generate ideas and optimize processes, but it is human creativity that will guide these tools toward meaningful, impactful, and innovative results.

As prompt engineers, content creators, designers, and professionals in any other field, embracing AI as a partner rather than a replacement will be key to thriving in this future. The relationship between AI and creativity is not one of competition—it's one of enhancement. The more effectively you can collaborate with AI, using your creativity to guide its outputs, the more you will be able to innovate, create, and shape the future in ways that are impossible without it.

In this AI-driven world, creativity isn't just something to be preserved in a human-only domain. It's something that can be enhanced, augmented, and expanded through our collaboration with AI. Together, AI and human creativity can open up realms of possibility that were once unimaginable. By embracing this partnership, we move into a future where the limits of what's possible are continually redefined, offering an exciting horizon for all those who dare to innovate.

THE ROLE OF CREATIVITY IN THE AI-DRIVEN FUTURE

As we step into a future where artificial intelligence is an integral part of daily life, it's easy to focus on the technical aspects—how AI works, what it can do, and how it can help optimize processes. However, amid all the technological advancements, one fundamental human characteristic remains crucial: creativity. In the AI-driven world, creativity isn't just important; it's indispensable. It's the thread that ties together data-driven outputs and meaningful, original work. In this section, we'll explore how creativity will shape the future of AI, particularly in areas like prompt engineering, content generation, art, and problem-solving.

Understanding the Symbiosis Between AI and Creativity

AI models, particularly those that are generative (like GPT for text or MidJourney for images), operate by recognizing patterns in vast datasets. These models can create text, images, and even music by predicting the next likely element in a sequence. They excel at generating responses based on input and learning from patterns, but the creative spark—the ability to come up with truly novel ideas, push boundaries, and inject meaning into something—remains distinctly human. This is where your role as a prompt engineer, creator, or developer becomes vital.

In essence, AI can be a catalyst for creativity, but it relies on you to provide direction. The creativity you bring to the table allows AI to generate outputs that are not just useful or functional, but also inspired and groundbreaking. For example, when creating an art piece using an AI image generator, you don't just give a basic prompt like "a forest." You add layers to it—"a mystical forest with fog and golden sunlight breaking through the trees"—to guide the AI toward something more specific, more vibrant, and more evocative. Without your creative input, the AI would simply generate generic images based on patterns it has learned, which might not be aligned with your vision.

Creativity in Prompt Engineering

In prompt engineering, the role of creativity is central to shaping how AI will respond. It's not just about knowing how to interact with an AI; it's about knowing how to communicate your vision clearly, concisely, and creatively. The more creatively you approach your prompts, the more effectively you can unlock the full potential of an AI model.

Consider the task of writing a story using an AI tool like GPT. If you simply ask the AI to "write a short story," the result might be passable, but it will lack flair, depth, or the personal touch that makes stories resonate with readers. However, by creatively crafting your prompt, such as "Write a short story about a detective in a futuristic city, who solves a crime using only the power of memory," you're able to guide the AI in a way that helps it generate an output that is not only cohesive but also engaging and fresh. Your creativity adds the critical layer of direction, making the result unique rather than generic.

The creativity here also lies in iterating your prompts. Sometimes the first result isn't quite right, and that's where human creativity shines. You can adjust the prompt to refine the output: "Now, make the detective a former psychologist, whose understanding of human behavior allows them to solve crimes in unconventional ways." This back-and-forth process of refining prompts, tweaking details, and iterating is a fundamentally creative act that elevates the AI-generated content into something extraordinary.

Creativity in AI-Assisted Design and Art

In fields like digital art and design, AI is already playing a transformative role. AI models can generate stunning visuals from simple text descriptions, creating everything from abstract designs to lifelike portraits. But, once again, it's the human creator who provides the vital spark of creativity. AI can provide inspiration and ideas, but it is the artist who interprets these ideas, adds context, and applies their unique perspective to the work.

For example, AI-generated images can serve as a starting point for a graphic designer working on a new logo. The designer might feed the AI specific keywords and instructions, and the model will generate several concepts based on those parameters. However, the designer's creativity is what takes those concepts and refines them, experimenting with colors, shapes, and proportions to create a final design that is not only aesthetically pleasing but also aligns with the company's branding and vision. In this way, AI doesn't replace the designer's creativity—it enhances it, offering new possibilities that wouldn't have been considered otherwise.

This kind of collaboration can be seen in the use of AI tools in music production as well. AI can help musicians by generating melodies, harmonies, or even lyrics based on a few input parameters. But, ultimately, the artist's creativity is what transforms those AI-generated pieces into complete compositions that evoke emotion, tell a story, and connect with listeners. The technology becomes a powerful tool in the creative process, expanding what is possible, but the artist's touch remains irreplaceable.

Creativity as a Catalyst for Innovation

As AI continues to evolve, it will increasingly become a tool that amplifies creativity, enabling new forms of innovation across industries. By using AI to automate repetitive tasks or generate initial drafts, creators can free up more time to focus on the aspects of their work that truly require human intuition and inspiration. This leads to more innovative outcomes, as creators are no longer bogged down by the mundane aspects of their tasks and can instead channel their energy into refining and exploring new ideas.

For instance, in the field of architecture, AI is being used to design buildings that are both structurally sound and visually unique. While the AI can help design efficient structures by analyzing building materials, weather patterns, and environmental factors, it's the architect who brings a sense of creativity to the project. They decide how to incorporate natural elements, cultural significance, and artistic vision into the design, resulting in buildings that are both functional and beautiful. In this case, AI acts as a tool that accelerates the design process, but it's the architect's creative thinking that leads to truly innovative results.

The Future of Creativity in AI Collaboration

Looking ahead, the role of creativity in AI is only set to expand. As AI models become more sophisticated, they will provide even greater opportunities for collaboration between humans and machines. But, despite these advancements, one thing remains certain: the human touch will continue to be essential. AI may be able to generate ideas and optimize processes, but it is human creativity that will guide these tools toward meaningful, impactful, and innovative results.

As prompt engineers, content creators, designers, and professionals in any other field, embracing AI as a partner rather than a replacement will be key to thriving in this future. The relationship between AI and creativity is not one of competition—it's one of enhancement. The more effectively you can collaborate with AI, using your creativity to guide its outputs, the more you will be able to innovate, create, and shape the future in ways that are impossible without it.

In this AI-driven world, creativity isn't just something to be preserved in a human-only domain. It's something that can be enhanced, augmented, and expanded through our collaboration with AI. Together, AI and human creativity can open up realms of possibility that were once unimaginable. By embracing this partnership, we move into a future where the limits of what's possible are continually redefined, offering an exciting horizon for all those who dare to innovate.

Thank you for reading this book!

I truly appreciate you taking the time to explore these pages. I hope the insights and ideas shared have inspired you to dive further into the exciting world of artificial intelligence and its creative applications.

Explore more!

I've put together a list of some of the leading AI generative tools that might be useful to you. Scan the QR code below to check it out and start experimenting.

Thank you once again, and happy exploring!

www.ingramcontent.com/pod-product-compliance
Lightning Source LLC
LaVergne TN
LVHW022346060326
832902LV00022B/4284